MW00900498

REDESIGNING SCHOOLS FOR *Success*

Implementing
Small Learning Communities
and
Teacher Collaboration

Charles E. Ruebling
with

Nancy A. Clarke   Frances A. Kayona   Shirley B. Stow

The Center for School Redesign™
A Division of The Ruebling Group, LLC
Longville, Minnesota
www.rueblinggroup.com/csr

AuthorHouse™
1663 Liberty Drive, Suite 200
Bloomington, IN 47403
www.authorhouse.com
Phone: 1-800-839-8640

AuthorHouse™ UK Ltd.
500 Avebury Boulevard
Central Milton Keynes, MK9 2BE
www.authorhouse.co.uk
Phone: 08001974150

ISBN: 1425959717 (soft)

Library of Congress Control Number: 2006908380

First published by AuthorHouse 10/02/06

Cover Design by Dan Seabreeze
Seabreeze Design
Peoria, Arizona

The One Page Business Plan® and The One Page ® are registered trademarks of The One Page Business Plan Company, Berkeley, CA.

Breaking Ranks II™ is a trademark of the National Association of Secondary School Principals, Reston, VA.

Balanced Leadership Framework™ and Leadership That Works™ are trademarks of Mid-continent Research for Education and Learning, Aurora, CO.

Printed in the United States of America
Bloomington, Indiana

This book is printed on acid-free paper.

i

Table of Contents

List of Figures and Tables

Acknowledgements

This is the first book project for us as a team. When reflecting on the well over 100 years of our collective work in schools, the names of many come to mind who personally taught, coached, encouraged, and criticized us as our careers were shaped, our skills were built, our passions were cultivated, our values were developed, and our ideas were tested. Without naming them here, we gratefully acknowledge their special gifts to us.

Then there are those with whom our primary interaction was as audience, of a book, tape, compact disc, lecture, or workshop. The Reference section identifies many of these individuals. To repeat a phrase that Doug Reeves used in a presentation, "These are the shoulders on which we stand." We are thankful for their contributions to our thinking and their contributions to the growth of educators nationally and internationally.

There are many who specifically helped to shape the ideas, content, and structure of this book. Valued friends and colleagues; Dennis Rens, Mary Lillesve, and Marvin Christensen; have given generously of their time discussing the contents of the book, making suggestions, and reading and commenting on manuscript drafts. Jim Horan gave valuable suggestions and feedback for the use of The One Page Business Plan®. We also had many opportunities to discuss the ideas in this book with educational leaders. They provided valued insights, suggestions, and encouragement. They are Latti Coor, Craig Paul, Chris Lennox, Margaret Leibfried, Maryann Nelson, Gaye Leo, Skot Beasley, Ann Orlando, Nancy Sharver, Janiene Marlow, Gary Ratigan, Jan Walker, Susan Garton, Angela Julien, Joy Wetzel, Dora Daniluk, Chad Teague, Cazilda Steele, Mary Kay Buehler, Sandra Wilson, Mary-Margaret Crandall and Vic Rinke. Sue Willer did an excellent job of editing the manuscript. Dan Seabreeze demonstrated his creativity and artistic talent in his design work. And the Team at AuthorHouse made publishing this book easy. To you all: THANK YOU!

A Vision for 21st Century Schools in America

Schools of the 21st Century in America will have increasingly higher expectations of ALL students, with ALL students achieving increasingly higher learning results. Schools will do this by redesigning themselves into Small Learning Communities of teachers, students, and parents who work collaboratively using the processes of planning, development, implementation, and evaluation focused on improving instruction, curriculum, assessment, and professional practice.

Preface

A Never Ending Journey

"It *is* the best of times; it *is* the worst of times." This present tense version of Charles Dickens' famous introduction to *A Tale of Two Cities* fits very well the situation in which public education finds itself today. One could say that it has always been this way. Over the last century, there have been many calls for improvement in our educational system. But no one can argue that public education in America has not gotten better. Today, it is better than it has ever been. So why can the situation in which public education finds itself also be called "the worst of times?"

The answer is quite simple. As public education has made its journey over the last century, the destination has not stood still. It keeps moving. The needs of learners in each succeeding generation change and increase, and public education must make adjustments to its *ends* and *means* in order to serve young people well.

As we look at the current situation, we can ask the question: Is public education adjusting fast enough to stay on course in its journey? Certainly the world situation in terms of politics, the environment, health, the economy, transportation, communication, and consumer needs and demands is creating new and more challenging problems to be solved. These problems, to be successfully solved, require new skills and capacities, not just for a few, but for *all* people. The changes and new needs are coming so fast that the requirements for increased knowledge and skills not only affect the young who are in K-12 public or private education; adults increasingly find themselves in situations where they must have new knowledge and skills to participate effectively in the workforce.

Today schools need to be more effective in preparing young people to participate meaningfully in life after high school. This challenge is not new. It is true, however, that the magnitude of the need has probably never been greater. The destination of the education journey is moving ahead faster than we are able to keep up; we need to make adjustments to the system that will speed progress and keep us on course. Redesigning systems in education is a fundamental requirement if new learning goals are to be met.

An Observation and a Question

This book project began when observations we made suggested that curriculum development was not followed by curriculum implementation (Ruebling, Stow, Kayona, and Clarke, 2004). Leaders were not leading with respect to the curriculum. There was little or no professional development focusing on the newly developed curriculum; there was little or no supervision of curriculum implementation; and there was little or no assessment data collected or examined regarding how well students were learning the new curriculum. Others had made this observation as well. Dufour (2005) notes that school districts that have made the effort to write curriculum often pay little attention to its implementation.

As we discussed these observations, we began thinking about other practices that our professional experience and reading suggested should be implemented in schools, but we were not seeing. Exploration of the literature led us to prominent educational researchers, experts, and organizations that were identifying these same practices as well as others. They noted that these practices, when implemented effectively, were related to increased student achievement. Yet, our observations as well as indications from the literature showed that these practices were not being implemented widely, effectively, or sustainably in most schools. The question was:

Why not?

Two factors came to mind: the *design* of the school and the *leadership* in the school. The notion that the design of an organization is related to its results (Senske, 2004) suggests that if schools are not achieving the desired results, perhaps a *redesign* would help. A redesign would, however, require leadership. Since the organization and structure of schools is much the same as it has been for a century (Burney, 2004), the needed leadership for redesign does not appear to be in place in most schools.

We hasten to say that there are examples of schools where the leadership has been effective in redesigning the organization and structure of the school. These examples tell us that the task is not impossible. The leadership literature suggests that effective leadership is learned behavior. We know that effective leadership is within the grasp of school leaders who are willing to make the effort.

This book is our attempt to offer guidance to education policy makers and leaders as well as teacher leaders, to help them make adjustments to the ways public education is organized and operated so that there can be greater success in moving forward on the journey and keeping on course.

Focus on the School

Our focus is at the school level. It is here that we believe more effective leadership is critical in order to change the organization and the operation of the school. We think this book will bring a new awareness and understanding to all those who have a stake in the education system of the need to redesign the organization and operation of the school. But, it is ultimately the leader of the school who must make it happen. Therefore, it is to these dedicated and hardworking men and women that we respectfully offer this book. We hope it will inspire them and give them new ideas that will help them lead their schools on the journey toward *all* students being successful learners.

Schools, however, do not operate in isolation. They are usually part of a larger organization, a school district and a community. School districts are "creatures" of state governments, which have constitutional authority and responsibility for effectively educating the young people of the state. Increasingly, the federal government has felt the need to exert influence on educational policy and practice. It does this by offering funding, but with "strings attached." So while the action, teaching and learning, is in the schoolhouse, the other levels of governmental authority have important roles and responsibilities for school success.

Is There Anything New?

Finally, it is important for us to say that much of what you will read here may not be new to you. You will note that we have used many sources. Our effort has been synthesis. We have taken the ideas of others, added some of our own, and put together a new "whole" which we have not seen fully implemented anywhere. Of course, that does not mean that it has not been implemented someplace. But we know the implementation is not widespread. Most schools are still organized and operated in essentially the same way they have been for decades. We are convinced that the 21st century requires something different.

The Authors
August 2006

Introduction

In light of the resource, social, political, and design realities facing our schools and their leaders, schools (as currently designed) are not likely to meet the expectations that no child be left behind.

(McREL, 2005, p. 7)

Why Redesign Schools?

This book is based on the assumption that schools in America, as they are currently *designed*, are unable to improve student achievement enough to meet the goals of No Child Left Behind by 2014, perhaps not ever. As Senske (2003) points out, "All organizations are perfectly designed to achieve the results they are getting" (p. 90). If the *results* an organization is getting are less than satisfactory, a *redesign* of the organization is needed. Elementary and secondary schools in America need to get better results. Senske goes on to say, "True organizational change begins by looking within and being open to the possibility of changing how we see ourselves, our working relationships, and the world in which we operate" (p. 90).

The problem is not that teachers and principals are not working hard; they are. The problem is that the way schools are organized and structured keeps teachers and students from reaching their full potential. The current organization of schools blocks principals and teachers from creating schools that are able to implement in sustainable ways the practices and concepts that research has found to be related to higher student achievement.

There is one statistic that gives a clear indication of the magnitude of the problem being faced by K-12 education today. "About 30% of high school freshmen never earn a diploma; figures are higher in urban districts" (Phi Delta Kappa, 2005, p. 1). The business community has also identified this problem. In an interview, Dr. Craig Barrett, Chairman of the Board of Intel Corporation, put it this way: "The most damning statistic is that

1

nationwide…roughly 30 percent of high school students never graduate from school. Think about that a moment – that's the workforce of the future! How can you take 30 percent of our young people and not give them basic rudiments of an education" (Meadors, 2005, p. 29)? Although this problem is often discussed in terms of a high school problem, the problem has its roots in K-8 education. The need is for a redesign of elementary, as well as secondary schools. Yet, as Burney points out: "The structure of schools and the assumptions under which they operate have not changed substantially in the past 100 years" (Burney, 2004, p. 527).

What is the problem with the current design? The current design features a single teacher, working alone, with individual responsibility for the learning of selected curriculum by a specified group of students. In elementary schools, the design is usually a single teacher, with a group of about 20 to 30 students, working in isolation from other teachers. The teacher is responsible for teaching all the subject areas to these students, with the probable exceptions of physical education, art, and music. In secondary schools, teachers usually have responsibility for teaching a single subject area (but sometimes two or three) and one or more courses within that subject area to 20 to 30 students at a time (sometimes more) in each of five to seven periods over the school day. Provisions are made for individual teacher preparation time, usually about 30 to 45 minutes in elementary schools and 45 to 60 minutes in secondary schools. The basic problem characteristics we see in the current design are (1) teachers working alone and in isolation; (2) a relatively small amount of teacher preparation time, alone; and (3) individual teacher responsibility for each student's learning. These characteristics inhibit the effective implementation of many instructional, curricular, and assessment practices that have been demonstrated to relate to increased student achievement and/or have been advocated by prominent educational organizations and individuals for decades. Another problematic issue with the current design is a "crowded curriculum" resulting from additions that have been made over many years with little being dropped. In many cases, the curriculum is not written and in most cases it is not aligned with state content standards. Assessment is also a problem. Assessment programs are based on one or a few, usually external, tests given at the end of the school year. These

2

tests may have questionable alignment with what is taught in the school and often they have not been made useful to teachers.

We recognize that this description of the problems with the current design may be a bit extreme. There are schools that are doing things differently, and the efforts of the leaders and staffs in some of these schools have rightfully been celebrated and honored. The research done in many of these schools is showing the way to improved achievement. But these schools are not the majority, and they usually do not represent the kind of comprehensive change that is proposed in this book and is needed for required growth in student achievement.

Practices and Concepts

We have identified "practices and concepts," which we will refer to simply as "practices" from this point forward, for inclusion in this book primarily from five major sources:

(1) *New Small Learning Communities: Findings from Recent Literature* (Cotton, 2004),

(2) *Breaking Ranks II™: Strategies for Leading High School Reform,* (NASSP, 2004),

(3) Effective Schools Research (Edmonds, 1979 and Taylor, 2002),

(4) *Effects of High School Restructuring: Ten Schools at Work* (Cawelti, 1997), and

(5) *Balanced leadership: What 30 years of research tells us about the effect of leadership on student achievement* (Waters, Marzano, and McNulty, 2003).

The practices that are emphasized in this book, along with the major reference sources used to support them, are listed in Figure I-1. They are grouped by the three major design elements of schools: instruction, curriculum, and assessment. A summary listing of the practices from each of these sources is given in Appendix A. Cotton's literature review identifies Key Elements of Success for small learning communities (SLC). For *Breaking*

Ranks II™, the list is made up of Seven Cornerstone Strategies and 31 Recommendations. Edmonds and Taylor identify Characteristics of Effective Schools. Cawelti identifies Seven Critical Restructuring Elements. For the Balanced Leadership Framework™, the list is 21 Leadership Responsibilities identified in the meta-analysis as positively and significantly correlated with student achievement. Although the *Breaking Ranks II*™ cornerstone strategies and recommendations and Cawelti's critical elements are based on high school literature and research, we believe that they can and should be applied in elementary schools as well as secondary schools.

Although we are mindful of Steven Covey's (1989) "begin with the ends in mind," we start with "means" (instruction), rather than "ends" (curriculum) as we lay out the practices. It is the school level instructional practices that provide opportunity for implementation of teacher level instructional practices and curriculum and assessment practices.

Elmore (1995) warns about assuming that structural changes will produce changes in teaching practices and student learning (as cited in Cawelti, 1997). This leads to a "chicken and egg" dilemma: Which should come first? Structural changes followed by changes in teaching practices? Or, changes in teaching practices followed by structural changes? We believe the problem is that the current organizational structure of teachers, students, and time prevents needed changes in curriculum, assessment, and instruction. We also recognize that changing organizational structure alone will not lead to changes in teaching practices. It is leadership's role to move beyond the organizational and structural changes; that is, to use them effectively to implement changes in instruction as well as in curriculum and assessment. As Cawelti (1997) points out, "Changes in school organization and structure are necessary in support of this goal [improved teaching and learning], but they have little value in and of themselves" (p. 11).

Figure I-1. Practices for School Improvement and Their Sources

Practices	Elements for Success of SLCs	Breaking Ranks II™ Strategies & Recommendations	Characteristic of Effective Schools	Critical Restructuring Elements	Balanced Leadership Responsibilities
School Level Instructional Practices					
Small Learning Community	X	X		X	
School-within-a-School	X	X			
Interdisciplinary Teaching Teams	X	X	X		
Common Preparation Time	X	X		X	
Teacher Leadership	X	X	X	X	X
Autonomy	X	X		X	X
Diverse/Heterogeneous Student Groups	X	X			
Looping	X	X			
Differentiated Staffing				X	
Teacher Level Instructional Practices					
Teacher Collaboration	X	X		X	
Continuous Professional Development	X	X		X	X
Personal Learning Plans (for teachers)		X			
Flexible Scheduling/Grouping	X	X			
Personalizing Students' Programs	X	X			
Personal Plan for Progress		X			
Personal Adult Advocates	X	X			
Family Involvement	X	X	X	X	
Curriculum Practices					
Curriculum Framework*					
Curriculum Development		X			X
Alignment with Content Standards		X			
Clearly Stated Vision and Mission Focused	X	X	X		
Essential Learnings and High Expectations		X	X	X	
Career Focus in All Courses		X			
Continuous Engagement in All Subject Areas,					
Curriculum Integration	X	X			
Assessment Practices					
Course Assessment Programs*					
Assessment Development					X
Alignment with Curriculum*					
Accountability	X	X		X	
Frequently Monitoring Achievement		X	X		X
Reporting Assessment Results		X			

* These practices are not found in the five major sources, but were added to the list based on the authors' experience

The *redesign* of elementary and secondary schools advocated in this book features, at the school level, *small learning communities* and *interdisciplinary teaching teams;* and at the teacher level, *teacher collaboration.* The implementation of these three practices opens the door of opportunity for many other practices that have been linked to increased student achievement; that is, school improvement. The question we raise is:

> *How can the organization and structure of schools be redesigned so that practices related to increased student achievement become sustainable parts of the regular, daily routine and culture of the school?*

Elements of School Design

Teacher collaboration in interdisciplinary teams is focused on the three major design elements of elementary and secondary schools:

1. Curriculum – the learning results the school is trying to achieve,
2. Assessment – how the school measures the learning results it is trying to achieve, the criteria for satisfactory performance, and the use of data obtained from those measures, and
3. Instruction – what the school and teachers do to achieve the learning results described in the curriculum and in the assessment program.

In this book, we emphasize the instructional element with respect to implementation ("how to"), but we also include important information about curriculum and assessment practices. It is not possible to discuss one design element without referring to the others in order to ensure that the critical quality of *alignment* of these three elements is honored. This alignment is displayed in Figure I-2, which also illustrates the concept of personalization from the student's point of view. In addition, the processes of teacher collaboration (planning, development, implementation, and evaluation) must be specifically directed toward improving the three design elements and toward the professional growth of teachers.

6

Figure I-2. Alignment of Curriculum, Assessment, and Instruction; Personalization of
Students' Educational Programs

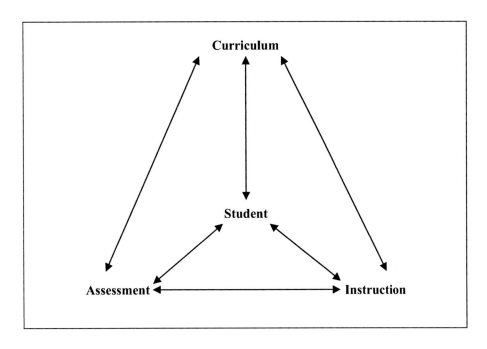

"Curriculum" is defined as a description of the learning results that the school is attempting
to achieve through instruction and measure through assessment. The curriculum is derived
from, and aligned with, state, national, and/or local content standards. As Reeves (2005b)
states, standards are not the equivalent of a useful curriculum. We take the point of view
that the curriculum, particularly in large schools, is over crowded and too broad in scope
for the time and dollar resources available for implementation. There is a need to rethink
the organization of the curriculum and the various subject areas in ways that support high
expectations for *all* students, curriculum integration, and the engagement of students with
all subject areas continuously from grades 1 through 12.

"Assessment" is defined as the collection of measurement instruments and processes that
are used to determine the extent to which the instructional element is successful at
producing the learning results described in the curriculum. The assessment program
establishes performance standards for satisfactory achievement. The "collection" of
measurement instruments and processes not only includes summative measures, it *must*
also include (1) measures taken during instruction that are "formative" in that they identify

learning problems early and (2) measures throughout the course that clearly indicate whether or not a student is on track for meeting the performance standard.

Assessment also includes the systems and processes for reporting, interpreting, and using the data obtained for purposes of accountability and instructional improvement. High quality assessment programs, which produce useful data for improving learning results as well as instruction, are not in place in most schools. Indeed, design and implementation of assessment and the use of assessment data continue to be neglected parts of teacher and principal preparation programs. We take the point of view that assessment should be focused at the *course level* with both internal (teacher constructed) and external (state constructed and commercially published) instruments. The assessment program needs to provide diagnostic, formative, and summative data that are reported to, and analyzed by, teaching teams.

Although assessment must first focus on learning results, it is important to have quality measures of the instructional processes that were used to obtain those results. These data inform the collaborative process of improvement (Reeves, 2002).

"Instruction" is defined very broadly as *all* the things a school and its teachers do that are directly intended to get the desired learning results described in the curriculum. This includes the organization of the teaching staff, students, and instructional time; leadership for teaching; systems, practices, and concepts that support the work of teachers; and instructional strategies and methods.

In the last few decades, much work has been done researching effective instructional pedagogy, strategies, methodology, and materials. (For example: Marzano, Pickering, and Pollock, 2001; Marzano, 2003, Cole, 1995) Much has been done to communicate this information to teachers and to train teachers in its application; still more needs to be done. Addressing specific issues of teaching methodology is beyond the scope of this book. Our emphasis relative to instructional practices is on the organization of teachers, students, and time and in discussing some specific school and teaching team practices related to individualizing and personalizing instruction.

Opportunity for School Improvement

Changing the design of the school relative to the organization of teachers, students, and time only creates the opportunity to implement other practices that are related to school improvement; that is, to increased student achievement. Changing the design relative to the organization of teachers, students, and time is necessary to "unlock the doors" of opportunity which the current design does not allow. Opportunity, however, does not automatically turn into results. It is necessary for the practices to be implemented effectively, and this is the challenge for school leadership, for the principal, superintendent, and others who play leadership roles in the school and district.

Feasibility of Redesign

Our exploration of redesigning elementary and secondary schools has also considered feasibility. We reviewed a study done by researchers at the Federal Reserve Bank of St. Louis (Hernandez-Murillo, and Roisman, 2004). They were investigating a possible relationship between student scores on the Missouri state mathematics test and student-to-teacher ratio and per pupil spending in 13 selected school districts in the St. Louis area. They concluded that there was not a relationship, but what intrigued us was the data about student-to-teacher ratio. The range was 11.5 to 17.2, and the median was 15.4. The source of these data was the National Center for Education Statistics (NCES) Common Core of Data for the 1999-2000 school year.

To examine what appeared to us to be very low student-to-teacher ratios, we looked at data housed at NCES for the 2003-2004 school year, which are now available. Specifically, we reviewed data of school districts that serve 49 state capital cities in America for which data were available. (See Appendix B for tables displaying these data.) We found the median

9

student-to-teacher ratio to be 15.2 with a range of 10.3 to 21.3. These ratios are students-to-teachers and do not include counselors, library/media specialists, or school nurses. The range of district enrollments was 1,065 to 109,424, not including one high-end outlier with enrollment of 183,609. These data caused us to ask this question:

What is a more effective way to organize the teacher resource already available in schools?

The redesign of elementary and secondary schools described in this book implements *small learning communities* consisting of *interdisciplinary teaching teams* and a relatively small group of students, in most cases. In this environment, effective *teacher collaboration* addressing instructional, curricular, and assessment practices related to increased student achievement and the professional growth of teachers is possible. The design does not require an increase of the teacher resource already available in schools, although schools with relatively high student-to-teacher ratios may need to be more creative in their approach. In this book, we describe one different, more effective way (not necessarily the only way) to organize the teacher resource already available in schools and to design instruction, curriculum, and assessment in ways that are more likely to achieve greater learning results.

Planning for Redesign of Schools

By definition, redesigning schools requires change of the current design, and change requires a plan for change. Schools go through strategic planning processes periodically. Efforts are made for broad, representative participation in the generation of needs, issues, recommendations, strategies, and action plans. The process usually produces large binders of materials that contain big plans for change. They are well intentioned, but frequently don't have a lot of meaning for most teachers. They usually don't change much that goes on in schools and classrooms. As Schmoker (2004) suggests, a new approach is needed; one which is short-term oriented in its objectives and action plans. We recommend and describe The One Page® concept for planning (Horan. 2004). This process creates

10

relatively brief plans written by the district superintendent, school principals, teaching team leaders, teachers, and students. Each one-page plan has a vision, mission, objectives, strategies, and action plans. While vision, mission, and strategies are longer term, objectives and action plans are annual or even less. The plans are aligned; their objectives are focused on learning; virtually all the key players participate; and participation deals specially with the responsibilities of the individual writing The One Page® plan. "Scorecards" are developed for frequently monitoring progress toward objectives. "Tracking charts" are developed for monitoring implementation of action plans. Plans are brief, reviewed frequently, and subject to adjustment when needed. Through the use of a relatively simple planning and performance system model, the redesign of the organization of teachers, students, and time; of instruction; of curriculum; and of assessment has a high probability of actually being implemented, and thereby increasing school success.

Overview of the Book

In Chapter 1, we introduce *school level* instructional practices that are related to increased student achievement and that are advocated by prominent educational organizations and experts. (See Figure I-1.) These practices are important *means* that can be used by the school and the school principal to achieve the *ends* described in the curriculum. For each practice, definitions and principles are given and application in a redesigned school is described.

In Chapter 1 these practices are discussed individually, although they are inter-related and should be implemented in concert. **Small learning communities** are created by forming **schools-within-a-school** featuring **interdisciplinary teaching teams** each having responsibility for a **diverse group of students**. Teaching teams have **common preparation time** together each day, develop their own **leadership**, and have **autonomy** for most instructional decisions for the students assigned to them. Teams have **differentiated staff** and remain with students for more than one year, a practice is known as **"looping."**

After introducing the practices that are implemented at the school level, an example of redesigning the organization of teachers, students, and time is given using a relatively simple school situation. This is an example of how teachers, students, and time can be organized to implement small learning communities and other important practices in a sustainable way. In Appendix C, we present more complex examples using data from real schools obtained from the NCES Common Core of Data. These examples vary in terms of student-teacher ratio, school enrollment, and the grade level organization of the school. The examples include elementary schools, middle level schools, and high schools.

Chapter 2 continues the discussion of instructional practices, but now is focused at the teacher level. First among these practices is *teacher collaboration*. Collaboration uses the processes of planning, development, implementation, and evaluation focused on improving instruction, curriculum, assessment, and the professional practice of team members. Teacher collaboration is important because in the complex environment of today's schools, one teacher working in isolation from colleagues cannot solve all of the instructional problems. Through **team collaborative** effort, **personalizing** the school environment for students becomes more feasible. Teachers focus their own **personal professional development** on the needs of the team and students. The educational program for students can become more individualized with **personalized plans for progress, personal adult advocates,** and **family involvement** in the educational process and decision-making.

Chapter 3 addresses the school design element of curriculum. The curriculum is written in the context of the school district's **vision and mission focused on student learning results.** Curriculum is **developed** using a **common curriculum framework** that creates curriculum documents that **align with state and/or national content standards,** have a **career focus** in all courses, and describe the **essential learnings**, which are **high expectations for all students.** Students have **continuous engagement** with all subject areas in grades 1 through 12. Interdisciplinary teaching teams make possible planned, systematic **curriculum integration**.

Chapter 4 deals with assessment. **Assessment development** is focused at the **course level** to ensure that teaching teams have data for **frequently monitoring student progress** toward performance standards and react quickly when problems occur. Assessment development **aligns instruments and exercises with the curriculum**. Assessment practices include the systems and processes for **accountability** and **reporting student progress**. These systems ensure that all who have a stake in the educational program have access to the information they need to make judgments and decisions that are accurate and appropriate.

Chapter 5 addresses leadership and strategic planning for implementation of the practices in the redesigned school. This chapter deals with the reality that *feasibility* and *research support* do not carry enough weight to make implementation a "slam-dunk." The reality is that redesigning a school, using the Balanced Leadership Framework™ (Waters, et al., 2003), is a "second order change" in most schools and for most people who work in schools. The change will profoundly affect "how business is done" in the school generally and for many individuals specifically.

We draw upon ideas about leadership and change from education and other fields to provide help and guidance for leaders working to redesign their schools for success by implementing small learning communities and teacher collaboration. Leaders should be humble yet tenacious (Collins, 2001) Leaders must set direction, develop people, and redesign the organization for collaboration (Leithwood, Louis, Anderson, and Walhstrom, 2004). Leaders must make decisions regarding what they will inquire about, focus on, monitor, and recognize (Reeves, 2005a). And leaders must continuously demonstrate knowledge and involvement in the design and implementation of curriculum, instruction, and assessment (Marzano, Waters, and McNulty, 2005).

Planning for change in schools is critical. It should be a simple, focused process that allows modification of plans during implementation. We describe The One Page® Strategic Planning Model (Horan, 2004) that creates plans with five components: vision, mission, objectives, strategies, and action plans. Individuals at the district, school, teaching team, teacher, and student levels write One Page Plans. Among the benefits of this planning process and tool are (1) plans are brief, changeable, and easy to monitor, (2) plans are focused on student learning, (3) plans are in alignment at all levels, (4) participation in the planning process is 100 percent, with participants writing plans that specifically address their responsibilities for achieving student learning results, and (5) it all fits on one page.

A Work in Progress

We see this book as a "work in progress." Districts and schools will need to tailor the ideas and recommendations they find in this book to their specific situations, but there are some principles that must be honored.

Our view of this book "project" is that it is the first of several. As follow-ups to this book we plan books specifically addressing "how to" build a useful curriculum that is aligned with state or national content standards and effectively guides assessment and instructional development, and "how to" build and select effective measuring instruments and exercises for course assessment programs. A third follow-up book will deal with establishing teacher collaboration processes of planning, development, implementation, and evaluation for improving instruction, curriculum, assessment, and professional practice. A fourth follow-up book will address the development and monitoring of The One Page® Plans for districts, schools, teaching teams, teachers, and students.

Chapter 1 – Creating
Small Learning Communities

Some [scholars, school leadership teams, and management experts] argue that most high schools are structured in a way that will not allow the change in culture necessary to adjust instruction to meet the needs of all students. Changing structures can be the first step in changing instruction and culture (although not the ultimate step).
(NASSP, 2004, p. 5)

Implement schedules that are flexible enough to…allow for effective teacher teaming and lesson planning.
(NASSP, 2004, p. 12)

Modify school schedules to include collaboration time for lesson planning and student work evaluation.
(O'Shea, 2005, p. 36)

Everyone in the educational community must work diligently to change structures that impede teamwork.
(Schmoker, 1999, p. 11)

In this chapter, we introduce school level instructional practices. These practices are strategies that schools (principals) can use to help students learn successfully. Although they have been in the literature for more than a decade, they have not been broadly implemented in schools in sustainable ways. In this chapter, we also introduce a new structure for the organization of teachers, students, and time that supports the sustainable implementation of these practices so that they can become part of the daily culture and routine of the school. These practices also create the opportunity for effectively implementing other important instructional, curricular, and assessment practices.

Instruction is defined as what the *school* and *teachers* do to achieve the learning results described in the curriculum. It is in the *school* that teaching and learning take place, or that direction is given for learning outside the walls of the school. The practices described in this chapter are school-wide, and the principal must take responsibility for their implementation. (In Chapter 2, instructional practices of teaching teams and teachers are presented.) These school-wide instructional practices relate to the organization and structure of teachers, students, and time. They are

1. Small learning communities,
2. Schools-within-a-school,
3. Interdisciplinary teaching teams,
4. Common preparation time for teaching teams,
5. Teacher leadership (distributed/shared leadership),
6. Autonomy (distributed/shared decision-making),
7. Diverse/heterogeneous student groups,
8. Looping, and
9. Differentiated staffing.

These practices, which establish the structure and conditions for the relationships that are created among and between teachers and students, are "enablers;" they create the opportunity for effective, sustainable implementation of the other instructional, curricular, and assessment practices that are implemented by teachers. At the school level, creating *small learning communities* consisting of *interdisciplinary teaching teams* and relatively *small groups of students representing the diversity in the school* is critical. These practices form the context for implementing the other supporting practices.

It must be noted that schools do not operate in isolation. In most cases, they are a part of a school district or larger private school organization that has policy and supervisory responsibilities with respect to its schools and the learning of students. It is important for school districts to have policies and regulations that support and encourage principals and teachers to use these practices.

Instructional Practices at the School Level

Prominent educational researchers, organizations, and/or experts support each of these nine school level practices as being related to increased student achievement. As these practices are discussed in the literature, they are not mutually exclusive. It is not unusual for one practice to have another as one of its defining or descriptive characteristics. Each practice, however, is given a separate section for discussion to facilitate understanding. Each practice will be discussed individually by giving *definitions and principles* and briefly describing the intended *application*.

Small Learning Community (SLC)

Definition and Principles

A *small learning community* is any separately defined, individualized learning unit within a larger school setting in which students and teachers are scheduled together (Sammon, 2000; as cited in Cotton, 2004). There is not complete agreement on what constitutes a small learning community in terms of students. While 500 seems to be the maximum, many writers put the number of students between 200 and 400 (Cotton 2004). Wyandotte (Kansas City, KS) High School organized into self-contained small learning communities of approximately 200 students that were schools-within-a-school taught by interdisciplinary teams of teachers (NASSP, 2004).

Small learning communities seem to improve the relationships among the members. Wasley observed a small learning community with eight teachers in Chicago: "Because they were few, they could meet together every day for an hour, work toward common agreements and understandings, and accept shared responsibility for their students. They discussed the curriculum in all subjects, agreed on instructional approaches, and tried to build as much coherence in the curriculum as they could manage" (Wasley, 2002, p. 10). Small units also improve the quality and quantity of student-teacher interaction (NASSP, 2004).

"Professional learning community" is another concept that has essentially the same characteristics as small learning community. DuFour (2005) discusses three "big ideas" that characterize professional learning communities: (1) ensuring that students learn, (2) a culture of collaboration, and (3) a focus on results. By example, he describes the collaborative work of five third grade teachers in a K-5 school serving 400 students that uses a process they call *team learning*, which includes (1) examining curriculum, (2) developing formative assessments and establishing standards, (3) examining the results of the formative assessments, (4) analyzing how well students have performed, (5) identifying strengths and weaknesses of student learning, and (6) discussing how to build on strengths and overcome weaknesses.

Small learning communities are not the cure for all the problems schools face. In their report on progress of small schools in Chicago, Wasley et al. state: "It is important to avoid seeing small schools as the sole solution to all that ails education. Rather, we would suggest that it is a key ingredient in a comprehensive plan to improve education" (as cited in Cotton, 2004, p. 5).

Application of *Small Learning Community*

The purpose of a small learning community is to create a group of teachers and students who are able to work closely together. The creation of small learning communities enables the effective and sustainable implementation of other important practices and realizes the benefits that research on small learning communities has identified.

For small learning communities that deal with the academic subject areas of Language Arts, Mathematics, Science, and Social Studies (Academic Small Learning Communities), the number of teachers and students is suggested to be eight to 12 teachers with about 200 students. In the ideal situation, the 200 students would be in a single grade level.

Small learning communities for two other groups of subject areas, which are called Personal Decision-Making and Fine Arts/Technology/World Languages, will have

18

considerably larger numbers of students assigned to them, often more than the 500 student limit suggested in the literature. The teams will work with larger numbers of students (as is the case with the current school design), but the *average* size of instructional groups with which teachers work at any given time during a school day is usually very similar to those of the Academic Small Learning Community.

The suggested number of students for Academic Small Learning Communities, about 200, needs to be put into the context of the existing parameters of a school including the number of students per grade level, grades included in the school, and student-to-teacher ratio. In schools with considerably fewer than 200 students per grade level, which may be the case in many elementary schools, multi-grade/age grouping is an option to obtain student groups of approximately 200. In schools with considerably more than 200 students per grade, the concept of school-within-a-school will be used to create more than one Academic Small Learning Community per grade level. Each small learning community is expected to be representative of the diversity of students in the grade.

Each small learning community is a *professional learning community* as well. The interdisciplinary team of teachers uses their collaborative work focused on instruction, curriculum, and assessment to identify professional learning needs of the team and its individual members. The team has responsibility for finding and implementing the professional growth activities to meet these needs. Professional growth activities may include workshop attendance, literature review, observation of other teachers, practice with feedback, etc., or probably, some combination of professional growth activities. The important point is that professional growth needs are directly related to problems that the team needs to solve. If the expertise for solving a problem or implementing a preferred solution is not present in the team members, obtaining the expertise through professional growth of team members is one option for getting it. Another option would be to use an internal or external consultant to obtain the expertise in the short term.

School-Within-a-School

Definition and Principles

A *school-within-a-school* (SWAS) operates within the context of a larger host school under the direction and supervision of the host school principal. The SWAS typically has its own teachers and students. The school's curriculum appropriate for the students in the SWAS is used. The SWAS may be organized by grade level; e.g., only third grade students, seventh grade students, 10th grade students, etc.; or vertically, multi-age/grade, to include two or more grades. In high schools, the concept may take on a career character being organized around career clusters or pathways (Cotton, 2004).

Application of *School-within-a-School*

The school-within-a-school concept is used to create small learning communities, and an entire school is divided into schools-within-a-school. Each has specific teachers and a specific group of students assigned to it. Teachers are assigned full-time whenever possible. These small learning communities must follow the curriculum (learning expectations) and assessment practices adopted by the district and school but have autonomy (and accountability) with respect to most instructional decisions. Common facilities of the school such as the cafeteria and library/media center are used by all schools-within-a-school, and all students are able to participate in the school's extra-curricular program. Each school-within-a-school has its own personnel, teaching and paraprofessional as well as others. Each school-within-a-school operates under the leadership and supervision of the principal.

Interdisciplinary Teaching Team

Definitions and Principles

Katzenback and Smith (1993) define *team* as "a small number of people with complementary skills who are committed to a common purpose, performance goals, and approach for which they hold themselves mutually accountable" (p. 45). Covey (2004) emphasizes the notion of complementary skills in a slightly different way when he describes a *complementary team* as one that has "a spirit of mutual respect so that the strengths of each are acknowledged and utilized, and the weaknesses are made irrelevant by the strengths of the others" (Covey, 2004, p. 213).

Schmoker (2005) writes: "Talent and sustained commitment are most apt to flourish in team settings that:

1. Combine autonomy *and* responsibility for results, and
2. Provide abundant opportunities for individuals to share their collective and complementary skills and abilities toward better results" (p. 146).

Blanchard, Randolph, and Grazier (2005) list these characteristics of a "next level team:"

1. Is a highly skilled, interactive group of people that uses the ideas and motivation of all team members
2. Uses information sharing to build high levels of trust and responsibility
3. Uses clear boundaries to create the freedom and responsibility to accomplish tasks in an efficient manner
4. Makes effective use of the time and talents of team members and their team leader
5. Uses self-managing skills to make team decisions and generate great results for the team, its members, and the organization (p. 7).

An interdisciplinary teaching team is a group of teachers who have a *common set of goals* (the curriculum assigned to the team), *shared responsibility and accountability* for the achievement of those goals by the students assigned to the team, and *diverse knowledge and skill* with respect to instruction, curriculum, and assessment. These characteristics are absolutely critical to the creation of a team. When a small group of people comes together to work toward common goals with mutual accountability, they, with good leadership, will very likely *build* themselves into an effective team.

One approach to organizing teaching teams, the one taken in this book, is to organize three types of interdisciplinary teams around subject areas: Academic, Personal Decision-Making, and Fine Arts/Technology/World Languages. The last team has three sub-teams, Fine Arts, Technology, and World Languages. Figure 1-1 shows how teachers with different subject area expertise have been grouped to create the three types of interdisciplinary teaching teams.

Figure 1-1. Subject Areas Assigned to Teaching Teams

Academic	Personal Decision-Making	Fine Arts/Technology/ World Languages
Language Arts	Health/Physical Education	Fine Arts
Mathematics	Family and Consumer Sciences	Technology
Science	Guidance	World Languages
Social Studies		

To maximize the effectiveness of the interdisciplinary teaching team, the qualities of "next level teams" listed by Blanchard et al., (2005) are cultivated under the leadership of the principal. The members of interdisciplinary teaching teams will develop the skills and attitudes necessary for (1) sharing ideas and information, (2) developing trust, (3) establishing and honoring group norms, (4) seeking to maximize the use of talents and expertise of individual team members, (5) making decisions by consensus, and (6) supporting each other in the generation of results.

Common Preparation Time for Teaching Teams

Definition and Principles

Common preparation time for a teaching team is a period of time when all members of the team can meet. To be effective and become a regular part of the school's routine and culture, the *opportunity* for teacher collaboration must be provided on a regular and frequent basis; daily.

Schools have used various approaches to provide common preparation time for groups of teachers. Some have created schedules that provide the time. Others have hired substitute teachers, used before or after school time, used staff development days, or sent students home early on selected days. One school took a more innovative approach. The principal, dean of students, counselor, and two paraprofessional staff supervised all the students (between 400 and 500) for the last 45 minutes of the school day once a week (Hall, 2005). The problems with these latter approaches are (1) they tend to be on the "fringe" of the organizational design and are usually unsustainable, (2) they don't provide enough time and the frequency of meetings is too low, (3) the groups that "collaborate" don't necessarily have common goals and shared responsibility for learning results, and (4) the common preparation time for teaching teams, which is required for teacher collaboration, does not become part of the routine culture of the school. For teacher collaboration to achieve its potential, these problems must be overcome.

Application of *Common Preparation Time for Teachers*

Common time together for teaching team members is intended for the collaborative implementation of the processes of *planning, development, implementation, and evaluation* focused on improving instruction, curriculum, assessment, and professional capacity and competence of teachers. One third of the students' school day, two hours in a typical six-hour school day, is committed to preparation time for each teaching team. It is the principal's leadership role to make sure that teachers, who may not be used to working collaboratively, learn how to use the common preparation time effectively and efficiently.

Increasing preparation time to one third of the school day for students is not intended to take the place of before and after school time, staff development days during the school year, and summer work time. The team's common time during the school day will include the entire team working together, subgroups within the team working together, as well as individual teacher preparation time. How the common preparation time is used is a team decision.

Teacher Leadership (Distributed/Shared Leadership)

Definition and Principles

In Cotton's (2004) review of small learning community literature, she states: "Leadership cannot be the exclusive purview of the principal...but must be assumed by teacher leaders as well" (p. 26). The principal must share leadership with teachers because the leadership required in schools demands more than one person can provide (McREL, 2005).

"Shared leadership implies shared responsibility and mutual accountability toward a common goal or goals for the good of the organization. Shared leadership is not a 'program' or a 'model.' It is a condition that can be enabled and sustained through organizational authority" (McREL, 2005, p. 71).

Recommendation 4 of *Breaking Ranks II*™ (NASSP, 2004) states: "Teachers will provide the leadership essential to the success of reform, collaborating with others in the educational community to redefine the role of the teacher and to identify sources of support for that redefined role" (p. 63). Further, a strategy suggested for this recommendation is to "move beyond the department head concept in order to cultivate leadership in teams" (p. 63). Teacher leadership goes beyond a teacher team leader. At times all teachers will take leadership roles because of their particular expertise or interest in a particular topic or situation.

Marzano, Waters, and McNulty (2005) recommend that principals distribute leadership responsibilities throughout the entire leadership team. Specifically, they suggest 12 of the 21 leadership responsibilities they found to be related to student achievement in their meta-analysis of research on principal leadership.

1. *Monitoring/Evaluating*: Monitors the effectiveness of school practices and their impact on student learning
2. *Knowledge of Curriculum, Instruction, and Assessment*: Is knowledgeable about current curriculum, instruction, and assessment practices
3. *Involvement in Curriculum, Instruction, and Assessment*: Is directly involved in the design and implementation of curriculum, instruction, and assessment practices
4. *Focus*: Establishes clear goals and keeps those goals in the forefront of the school's attention
5. *Intellectual Stimulation*: Ensures that the faculty and staff are aware of the most current theories and practices and makes the discussion of these a regular aspect of the school culture
6. *Flexibility*: Adapts his or her leadership behavior to the needs of the current situation and is comfortable with dissent
7. *Resources*: Provides teachers with materials and professional development necessary for the successful execution of their jobs
8. *Contingent Rewards*: Recognizes and rewards individual accomplishments
9. *Outreach*: Is an advocate and spokesperson for the school to all stakeholders
10. *Discipline*: Protects teachers from issues and influences that would detract from their teaching time and focus
11. *Change Agent*: Is willing to and actively challenges the status quo
12. *Order*: Establishes a set of standard operating procedures and routines.

Application of *Teacher Leadership (Distributed/Shared Leadership)*

Teaching teams need leadership services. Although these services must initially come from the school leader (the principal), the goal is to have leadership services emerge from the team itself; from teachers.

The principal sharing leadership responsibility with the teacher leaders is critical to the effective implementation of teacher leadership. Each team will have a team leader who is a teacher. The principal may select the team leader using a process that treats all willing candidates fairly, or the team may select its leader from the membership of the team. The teacher leader will provide leadership services to the team's operation, including facilitating meetings, representing the team at school leadership meetings, and administering the team's resources (budget, facilities, time). The teacher leaders of the small learning communities become members of the school leadership team. The principal will distribute the 12 leadership responsibilities as recommended by Marzano et al. (2005).

Sharing these leadership responsibilities with teaching team leaders (and perhaps others in the school) does not mean that the principal gives up her or his own responsibility in these areas. Initially, the principal must be sure of the capacity and competence of teacher leaders relative to each leadership responsibility before sharing that leadership responsibility with them. Ongoing, the principal will continue to frequently monitor and supervise the work of teams as well as demonstrate these responsibilities in his or her own work in the school.

Autonomy (Distributed/Shared Decision-Making)

Definition and Principles

Autonomy is created when decision-making is distributed (or shared, or delegated) to others. The purpose is to assign decision-making to the parts of an organization that are

26

most directly in contact with the work (teaching) and customers/clients (students and parents) of the organization. By doing so, decision-making is improved because the decision-makers have expertise and access to information not readily available to more central parts of the organization. In addition, according to Duke and Trautvetter, "Units that enjoy a high degree of autonomy are more likely to generate a unique culture and an inspired commitment to the success of the program" (as cited in Cotton 2004, p. 17).

Reeves (2005a) in discussing "an alternative vision of leadership effectiveness," describes leadership as decision-making in four essential areas: inquiry, focus, monitoring, and recognition. With this vision, distributed/shared decision-making and distributed/shared leadership are closely related. Note that Reeves' four areas for leadership decision-making are included in the 12 leadership responsibilities that Marzano et al. (2005) recommend distributing to, and sharing with, the leadership team of the school. By sharing leadership activities and responsibilities; i.e., sharing decision-making; the principal creates an environment that is more likely to maximize the strengths of individuals and teams (McREL, 2005).

Wohlstetter, Smyer, and Albers Mohrman concluded that site-based management (also known as distributed decision-making) as a governance reform can create the opportunity for school improvement only if it is combined with reforms in instruction (as cited in Cawelti, 1997). Instructional reform must involve reform at the teacher-student level. The important point is that one should expect that instruction will change for the better when those closest to the implementation of instruction are making important decisions.

Application of *Autonomy (Distributed/Shared Decision-Making)*

Principals will delegate decisions regarding instruction of students, the *means* used to achieve the *ends* described in the curriculum documents, to the teaching teams. This delegation is made with the understanding that decisions must always (1) be within the policies set by the board of education and regulations of the district and school, (2) give consideration to good teaching practices, and (3) have a "cooperative spirit" with respect to other teachers and students working in the school. The instructional decision-making over which teaching teams are given autonomy includes such areas as use of money that has been allocated for materials, supplies, staff training; type of support staff needed (e.g., instructional aides, substitute teachers, volunteers); use of the time in the school day that is assigned to the team; instructional methodology; and solutions to instructional problems.

Note that autonomy for decision-making with respect to the learning expectations of students described in the curriculum; i.e., the *ends* of education; is *not* delegated to teaching teams. Nor are they the purview of the principal. The curriculum is established by state and local policy; i.e., state and local content standards and the district's curriculum documents; which principals and teachers are obligated to accept. Although as subject matter experts teachers participate in the preparation of content standards and curriculum documents, the process by which they are established is political. They may not always be what teachers and principals would like them to be.

It must be clear that when teaching teams are given autonomy by the principal relative to instructional process, it is *delegation*, not *abdication*. The principal has not lost accountability for *results*, nor has the principal given up the responsibility to supervise instruction. The principal's supervision must include asking the question "why" a certain decision was made and require that the rationale be sound.

In a recorded seminar, Covey (2004) points out an important distinction between accountability for *process* and accountability for *results*. The principal maintains, and shares, accountability for results with the teaching team. But accountability for teaching strategies and methods lies with the teaching team; the teaching team is accountable to the principal for these processes. The team is responsible/accountable for selecting the best teaching practices available to accomplish curricular goals, for solving instructional problems, and for executing the solutions effectively.

Diverse/Heterogeneous Student Groups

Definition and Principles

Diverse/heterogeneous refers to the mix of students in a group. To be heterogeneous, the student group must reflect the diversity of the community being served by the school in terms of social, economic, racial, and ethnic characteristics. It must also reflect the diversity of learning abilities found in the school and at grade levels.

Application of *Diverse/Heterogeneous Student Groups*

The intention is that students assigned to teaching teams represent the diversity of the school population relative to gender, race, ethnicity, socio-economic status, and learning abilities. Copland and Boatright (2002) point out that diverse/heterogeneous grouping of students is beneficial when leaders walk the talk of social justice and equity:

> The small school movement responds to this issue of educational inequality by offering historically underserved populations an opportunity to flourish and grow in settings where teachers know and care about them. In successful small schools...there is greater emphasis placed on effectively addressing the learning needs of every student (p. 765).

This "intention" may be controversial. There is considerable evidence as well as the support of prominent educational organizations and experts for heterogeneous grouping. In some communities, however, there is strong pressure for grouping that is more homogeneous. (For example, Evans, 2003.) In either case, it is probable that implementation of small learning communities where interdisciplinary teams of teachers collaborate in planning, developing, implementing, and evaluating instruction will lead to raising achievement levels.

Looping

Definition and Principles

Fine and Summerville define *looping* as "having one group of teachers remain with the same students over time" (as cited in Cotton 2004, p. 24). Cotton (2004) goes on to point out that practitioners and researchers have found that in successful small learning communities students often remain with the same teachers for multiple years. "This arrangement ensures that students will be known well by more than one adult and is conducive to the formation of a community of learners" (p. 24). "Students may benefit from a looping structure that enables them to build trust and take more academic risks than they might with a teacher who disappears after one semester or even one school year" (Copland and Boatright, 2004, p. 764).

By creating multi-year relationships between an interdisciplinary teaching team and a relatively small group of students, the complicating factor of meeting, learning about, and understanding an entirely new group of students each school year is removed. Looping is a "simplifying factor" for the work of teachers.

Application of *Looping*

Looping is implemented in the school with small learning communities remaining together for up to four years. The grade levels present in the school and the number of students will affect the length of time or the number of years that students and teachers are "looped together." At the high school level, grades 9 and 10 and grades 11 and 12 are grouped together; looped. However, for grade 11 and 12 the issue of "career focus" for students may require changes of teacher expertise on the team.

Looping has a simplifying effect for teachers by maintaining established student-teacher relationships over several years. It can also be argued that there is a complicating effect because the curriculum changes from year to year as students progress through the grades.

30

We believe that in districts that have well-written curricula (as described in Chapter 3), this potential complication is mitigated. In addition, we advocate for teacher specialization in only one subject area, probably two at the elementary level. This will provide the knowledge background necessary for teaching a broader section of the subject area than is typically found in one school year.

Differentiated Staffing

Definition and Principles

Differentiated staffing refers to different categories and levels of jobs that are assigned to accomplish a goal. Significant goals are usually sufficiently complex to require different kinds of expertise or specialized knowledge and skill. Some specialized knowledge and skill may be the primary function needed while other specialized knowledge and skill may support the primary function. To operate effectively and efficiently, the various jobs, and the individuals holding those jobs, must coordinate their work in a timely fashion.

Instruction is what schools and teachers do to facilitate and support the work of students, which is learning. There are many tasks and a broad set of knowledge and skills necessary to deliver effective instruction, particularly in the increasingly complex environment in which schools operate today. All schools differentiate among some tasks, particularly along the lines of the primary work of teaching; e.g., explaining concepts to students; and work that supports teaching; e.g., copying handouts or cleaning classrooms. Traditionally, a single teacher has been expected to do all of the primary teaching tasks and many of the support tasks. As Trump (1977) pointed out some time ago, many of the tasks that are expected of teachers do not utilize the unique knowledge and skill of teachers and, therefore, waste their time.

As the learning environment and the tasks of teaching have become more complex, it becomes more difficult to create and maintain high levels of knowledge and skill in a single person, a single teacher. Increasing differentiation of the teaching role/work through teacher specialization in subject areas and special instructional methods related to student characteristics is necessary to bring higher levels of competence to bear on the problem of implementing effective teaching.

Using terminology that is probably familiar to educators, categories and levels of jobs in schools related to teaching include teacher, teacher intern, teacher leader, counselor, special education teacher, gifted and talented teacher, library/media specialist, school nurse, substitute teacher, student teacher, paraprofessional, instructional aide, and volunteer.

Application of *Differentiated Staffing*

Each teaching team will have members with complimentary specializations and support staff. Each team will have a teacher leader. Beyond this, there is *opportunity* for differentiation of staff by having categories of teachers such as master teacher, career teacher, beginning teacher, substitute teacher, teacher intern, and student teacher. Such categorizations must be clearly and meaningfully defined in terms of differentiated knowledge and skill levels, differentiated expectations relative to contribution to goal achievement, and compensation.

Teaching teams have a relatively high degree of autonomy with respect to instructional decisions. Therefore, each team will create its own pattern of differentiation. The starting point for differentiation of staff, however, includes a teacher leader, teachers with different subject matter expertise, teachers with different instructional expertise (e.g., special education), and instructional aides or paraprofessionals.

Organizing Teachers, Students, and Time for Small Learning Communities

With these nine practices in mind, we turn to the organizational and structural design of a school that will allow them to be implemented and sustained over time. The organizational and structural design features **small learning communities** created by forming **schools-within-a-school** which are **interdisciplinary teaching teams** with **differentiated staffing** and **teacher leaders.** The teaching teams (1) work exclusively with a relatively small, **heterogeneous group of students** over several school years **(looping)**, (2) have considerable **autonomy** for decisions related to instruction and professional growth, and (3) have **common preparation time** each school day.

To illustrate this design, a fictional school district with relatively simple parameters is used. The fictional school district, Columbia School District, has three schools: Columbia Elementary School, Columbia Middle School, and Columbia High School. Each school has four grades and 200 students enrolled in each grade.

These organizational and structural changes are not applied to kindergarten. The student-to-teacher ratio excluding kindergarten students and teachers but including counselors, library/media specialists, and school nurses is 15.1 to 1. This is comparable to the 15.2 to 1 median of the school districts that serve capital cities in the 49 states for which data were available from the National Center for Education Statistics (NCES) for the 2003-2004 school year. (See Appendix B for tables containing the NCES data for schools serving state capital cities.) Note that the student-to-teacher ratios found in the NCES data do not include counselors, library/media specialists, or nurses.

With respect to the number of instructional aides assigned to schools in the Columbia School District, we used the median, 4.2, teacher-to-instructional aide ratio found in the 49 school districts that serve capital cities. The range of teacher-to-instructional aide ratio was 1.7 to 9.2.

In Appendix C, there are illustrations of the redesign of teacher and student organization and the structure of time. These illustrations vary student-to-teacher ratio up to 20 to 1, use different grade level organizations, and vary the number of students at a grade level. The numerical parameters for these illustrations come from actual school data in the NCES Common Core of Data. For these illustrations, we make the assumptions that the grade

33

organization in a school district cannot be changed and that the student-to-teacher ratio in a school cannot be lowered; the design must work with the number of teachers that exists. This is the reality we assume: It is unlikely that schools will receive new funds in amounts significantly greater than the rate of inflation, and, therefore, a significant increase in the number of teachers is unlikely. As the student-to-teacher ratio goes up, the average size of instructional groups of students naturally goes up. In schools with higher than the median student-to-teacher ratios now, those numbers are already higher. We believe that even when student-to-teacher ratios are higher, the benefits gained from a design that supports small learning communities and common preparation time for interdisciplinary teaching teams to work collaboratively outweighs the compromises that must be made because of higher student-to-teacher ratios and more complex school parameters.

Figures 1-2 and 1-3 show the data for the fictional Columbia School District that are comparable to the NCES Common Core of Data. (Note that kindergarten is not included. This will be the case with all illustrations in Appendix C as well.) For the Columbia School District, there are 200 kindergarten students with 10 teachers assigned to them. In this case, we are assuming an "all day" kindergarten program with a student-to-teacher ratio of 20 to 1. In all illustrations, we assume that kindergarten will be operated as it has been in the past and do not include kindergarten teachers or students.

Figure 1-2. Columbia School District - School District Data

Number of schools	3
Enrollment (including kindergarten students)	2600
FTE classroom teachers (including kindergarten teachers)	157.0
Student-teacher ratio*	16.6
Elementary counselors	2.0
Secondary counselors	4.0
Library/media specialists	3.0
Instructional aides	39.0
Teacher-instructional aide ratio	4.2
Student support services (School nurses)	3.0
District administrators	3.0

* Does not include counselors, library/media specialist, and school nurses

Figure 1-3. Columbia School District - School Data

Schools	Elementary School				Middle Level School				High School				District
Grades*	1	2	3	4	5	6	7	8	9	10	11	12	Total
Students*	200	200	200	200	200	200	200	200	200	200	200	200	2400
Teachers*	49				49				49				147
Counselors	2				2				2				6
Lib/Media	1				1				1				3
Nurse	1				1				1				3
Instr. Aides	12				12				12				36
Tch/Instr.Aide	4.1				4.1				4.1				4.1
Sch. Admin.	2				2				2				6
Dist. Admin.													3
Student/Tch.	15.1				15.1				15.1				15.1

* Excludes Kindergarten: 10 teachers, 3 instructional aides, and 200 students

Interdisciplinary Teaching Teams

The interdisciplinary teaching teams in the Columbia School District schools are organized around three major subject area groups as shown in Figure 1-1 on page 22: Academic, Personal Decision-Making, and Fine Arts/Technology/World Languages. The last team has three subgroups of Fine Arts, Technology, and World Languages. These subject area groups were created using essentially the subject areas that are found in most schools today. (The subject area groups are discussed further in Chapter 3 where the rationale for the groups is presented.) In Columbia School District, World Languages are offered only at the high school, as is the case in many school districts.

Figures 1-4, 1-5, and 1-6 show the interdisciplinary teams with differentiated staffing for Columbia Elementary School, Columbia Middle School, and Columbia High School, respectively. In addition to regular education teachers and special education teachers, each team has instructional aides assigned to it. Because of the simple parameters we have chosen, the organizational structure for teachers and students is nearly the same in each school.

Student-to-teacher ratios for teams are calculated using the number of students assigned to the team divided by the sum of regular education teachers, special education teachers, counselors, library/media specialists, and nurses assigned to the team. Counselors, library/media specialists, and nurses are included in these counts because they will be scheduled with groups of students regularly to deliver instruction for curriculum assigned

Figure 1-4. Columbia Elementary School – Teaching Teams

Academic Grade 1 200 students	Academic Grade 2 200 students	Academic Grade 3 200 students	Academic Grade 4 200 students	PDM Grades 1-4 800 students	FA/T/WL Grades 1-4 800 students
Teachers with Subject Area/Instructional Specialization					
Language Arts Language Arts Mathematics Mathematics Science Science Social Studies Social Studies Special Education	Language Arts Language Arts Mathematics Mathematics Science Science Social Studies Social Studies Special Education	Language Arts Language Arts Mathematics Mathematics Science Science Social Studies Social Studies Special Education	Language Arts Language Arts Mathematics Mathematics Science Science Social Studies Social Studies Special Education	Health/Phys. Ed.* Health/Phys. Ed. Health/Phys. Ed. F&C Science* F&C Science Counselor Counselor Nurse Special Education	Visual Art Visual Art Music Music Technology Technology Lib./Media Spec*. Special Education
Student-to-Teacher Ratios					
9 FTE * teachers S/T* = 22.2	9 FTE teachers S/T = 22.2	9 FTE teachers S/T = 22.2	9 FTE teachers S/T = 22.2	9 FTE teachers S/T = 88.9	8 FTE teachers S/T = 100.0
				17 FTE teachers S/T = 47.1	
Paraprofessionals					
Instructional Aide Instructional Aide	Instructional Aide Instructional Aide	Instructional Aide Instructional Aide	Instructional Aide Instructional Aide	Instructional Aide Instructional Aide Health Aide Counselor Aide	Instructional Aide Instructional Aide Media Aide

* FTE = full-time equivalent, S/T = student-to-teacher ratio, F&C Science = Family and Consumer Science, Phys. Ed. = Physical Education, Lib./Media Spec. = Library/Media Specialist

Figure 1-5. Columbia Middle School – Teaching Teams

Academic Grade 5 200 students	Academic Grade 6 200 students	Academic Grade 7 200 students	Academic Grade 8 200 students	PDM Grades 5-8 800 students	FA/T/WL Grades 5-8 800 students
Teachers with Subject Area/Instructional Specialization					
Language Arts Language Arts Mathematics Mathematics Science Science Social Studies Social Studies Special Education	Language Arts Language Arts Mathematics Mathematics Science Science Social Studies Social Studies Special Education	Language Arts Language Arts Mathematics Mathematics Science Science Social Studies Social Studies Special Education	Language Arts Language Arts Mathematics Mathematics Science Science Social Studies Social Studies Special Education	Health/Phys. Ed. Health/Phys. Ed. Health/Phys. Ed. F&C Science F&C Science Counselor Counselor Nurse Special Education	Visual Art Visual Art Music Music Technology Technology Lib./Media Spec. Special Education
Student-to-Teacher Ratios					
9 FTE teachers S/T = 22.2	9 FTE teachers S/T = 22.2	9 FTE teachers S/T = 22.2	9 FTE teachers S/T = 22.2	9 FTE teachers S/T = 88.9	8 FTE teachers S/T = 100.0
				17 FTE teachers S/T = 47.1	
Paraprofessionals					
Instructional Aide Instructional Aide	Instructional Aide Instructional Aide	Instructional Aide Instructional Aide	Instructional Aide Instructional Aide	Instructional Aide Instructional Aide Health Aide Counselor Aide	Instructional Aide Instructional Aide Media Aide

Figure 1-6. Columbia High School – Teaching Teams

Academic Grade 9 200 students	Academic Grade 10 200 students	Academic Grade 11 200 students	Academic Grade 12 200 students	PDM Grades 9-12 800 students	FA/T/WL Grades 9-12 800 students
Teachers with Subject Area/Instructional Specialization					
Language Arts Language Arts Mathematics Mathematics Science Science Social Studies Social Studies Special Education	Language Arts Language Arts Mathematics Mathematics Science Science Social Studies Social Studies Special Education	Language Arts Language Arts Mathematics Mathematics Science Science Social Studies Social Studies Special Education	Language Arts Language Arts Mathematics Mathematics Science Science Social Studies Social Studies Special Education	Health/Phys. Ed. Health/Phys. Ed. F&C Science F&C Science Counselor Counselor Nurse Special Education	Visual Art Visual Art Music Music Technology World Languages World Languages Lib./Media Spec. Special Education
Student-to-Teacher Ratios					
9 FTE teachers S/T = 22.2	9 FTE teachers S/T = 22.2	9 FTE teachers S/T = 22.2	9 FTE teachers S/T = 22.2	8 FTE teachers S/T = 100.0	9 FTE teachers S/T = 88.9
				17 FTE teachers S/T = 47.1	
Paraprofessionals					
Instructional Aide Instructional Aide	Instructional Aide Instructional Aide	Instructional Aide Instructional Aide	Instructional Aide Instructional Aide	Instructional Aide Instructional Aide Health Aide Counselor Aide	Instructional Aide Instructional Aide Media Aide

to their respective teams. (See Chapter 3 for a discussion of the Guidance curriculum of the American School Counselor Association, the Information Literacy Standards of the American Association of School Librarians and the Association for Educational Communications and Technology, and the Health Teaching Standards of the National Association of School Nurses.) Generally, the target for these ratios in any school ranges from 20 to 30 (depending on the current overall district or school student-to-teacher ratio) for Academic Teams and approximately twice the Academic Team ratio for the combined Personal Decision-Making and Fine Arts/Technology/World Languages Teams. The *average* size of instructional groups is very similar across all three types of teams because the Personal Decision-Making (PDM) Team and the Fine Arts/Technology/World Languages (FA/T/WL) Team work with only half the students during a two-hour block of time.

Although the Academic Teams are assigned 200 students, the Personal Decision-Making and Fine Arts/Technology/World Languages teams have much larger numbers of students assigned to them. In the case of Columbia School District, these two teams in each school have all 800 students enrolled in the school assigned to them. This is generally the case in schools today with some variation due to some subject areas being elective or not required in each semester or school year. (In Chapter 3, we discuss issues related to required and elective curriculum in the context of the "continuous engagement" curriculum practice.)

In reality, each of the teachers in each of the three subject areas of the Personal Decision-Making group will need to work with only half of the students, 400. There are two teachers for each subject area, so they can divide the students if they choose. A similar situation occurs in the Fine Arts/Technology/World Languages group. Although it may be desirable to have smaller numbers of students assigned to these two teams, this is a practical compromise necessary to work within the parameter of the total number of teachers available. We believe that the benefits of small learning communities, interdisciplinary teaching teams, and common preparation time justify the compromise.

The membership of teaching teams is differentiated. Teachers have specific subject area expertise, such as science, or instructional expertise, such as special education. The team also has non-teacher members, instructional aides. They perform various non-teaching functions and, under a teacher's direction and with proper training, some teaching and student supervision functions. Here are more specific comments about the various roles and staff included on the teaching team.

Academic Team Teachers: Although teachers on the Academic Teams are labeled as two each for Language Arts, Mathematics, Science, and Social Studies, the elementary level will probably place greater emphasis for instruction on Language Arts and Mathematics. In that case all regular education teachers may work with students in Language Arts and Mathematics. Given the nature of Science curriculum and instruction, it will probably be important at the elementary level to have teachers who specialize in Science deliver all of the Science instruction. In middle and high schools, teachers belonging to the Academic Teams usually specialize in a single subject area, but sometimes more than one.

Personal Decision-Making Team Teachers: Personal Decision-Making Teams include teachers with subject matter expertise in Health and Physical Education, Family and Consumer Science, and the Guidance curriculum. Teacher members of this team include counselors and school nurses. (The team could also include individuals with titles such as psychologist, social worker, dean of students, and assistant principal for discipline.) Counselors and school nurses teach the curriculum related to their expertise (Guidance and Health, respectively) to groups of students and work individually with students who have special needs that require a one-on-one approach to teaching or assessment.

Fine Arts/Technology/World Languages Teachers: Teachers assigned to this team are further divided into three subgroups because of the differences in the subject areas. The subgroups are Fine Arts, Technology, and World Languages. The teachers, however, must all work together to schedule and to group students. Library/media specialists are included on this team in the Technology subgroup and are responsible for teaching the curriculum related to their expertise; information literacy The library/media center may serve as a place where students work independently in small groups or individually during the block of time assigned to this team. Other technology teachers are those who have traditionally been part of the vocational programs. As these programs have adapted to changing times and technology, the content has moved toward information systems and computer supported manufacturing and design techniques. Technology curriculum now includes application of modern technology to business, manufacturing, and service industries. World Languages teachers may not be present on teams in elementary and middle schools.

Special Education Teachers: It is assumed that ten percent of the students assigned to each team will have Individual Educational Plans (IEP) as defined by special education laws and policies. It is also assumed that these students are "mainstreamed" with regular education students whenever possible under the "least restrictive environment" policy. Special education teachers are assigned to each teaching team. Their role as team members is both assisting regular education teachers in their work with special education students and delivering instruction. The special education teachers are responsible for managing the IEPs of special education students.

Special Education Teacher Certification: Certification for special education teachers is by individual categories of special education students, with some multi-categorical certification. Probably the special education students assigned to any one teaching team will represent more than one category. This raises several questions: How will appropriate services be provided to special education students when the one special education teacher on the team has only one categorical certification? There is also the issue of "resource room" services for students when "mainstreaming" is not appropriate. How can the resource room be accommodated? The interdisciplinary teaching teams and the type of school schedule proposed help to address these issues. First, more than one Academic Team will have the same preparation time. This provides a opportunity of special education teachers with different categorical certification/expertise to consult with each other and with other teaching teams. With respect to resource rooms, special education teachers could be scheduled as a resource room teacher as the needs arise.

Instructional Aides: Each teaching team is assigned instructional aides. The team is responsible for directing their work. The intention is for instructional aides to (1) relieve teachers of clerical tasks, (2) provide instructional services, after appropriate training and as directed by teachers, and (3) supervise students in situations such as individual/group independent work, recess activities, physical education locker rooms, etc., again, with appropriate training.

Health Aides: In addition to instructional aides assigned to the Personal Decision-Making Team, a health aide is assigned to operate the Health Center of the school under the direction of the school nurse.

Counselor Aides: In addition to instructional aides assigned to the Personal Decision-Making Team, a counselor aide is assigned to operate the Counseling Center of the school under the direction of the counselors.

Media Aides: In addition to instructional aides assigned to the Fine Arts/Technology/ World Languages Team, a media aide is assigned to operate the Library/Media Center of the school under the direction of the Media Specialist.

Substitute Teachers: Though not shown in the figures illustrating the teams, each teaching team may be assigned specific substitute teachers. When a team has a need for a substitute teacher, the call would first go to one of those assigned to the team. This addition to the staff assigned to a teaching team would have the benefit of each substitute teacher becoming familiar with the assigned team's operation and students, making possible more productive and effective use of substitute teachers when necessary. The teaching team makes decisions regarding when and how to use substitute teachers, which could include participation in team planning, development, implementation, and evaluation activities.

Volunteers: Not shown in the figures, each teaching team is expected to recruit volunteers from among the students' parents and other community members. Volunteers would work under the direction of the teaching team and within the school district's policies regarding volunteers.

The School Schedule

The time structure for each of the schools in the Columbia School District allocates two thirds of the students' school day to the Academic Group of subject areas. The remaining one third of the students' school day is allocated to the Personal Decision-Making and Fine Arts/Technology/World Languages Groups of subject areas and to student independent work time.

Figure 1-7 gives three examples of what the school schedule could look like. These schedules assume a school day of six hours plus a lunch period. These school schedules provide a two-hour block of common preparation time for each teaching team each day. This block of time ensures the *opportunity* for the team to work together as part of teachers' daily routine. Lunch periods would be scheduled to accommodate the capacity of the cafeteria facility and the appropriate placement around the noon hour in the school day.

Figure 1-7. School Schedules

Periods	Grade A	Grade B	Grade C	Grade D
1	PDM – FA/T/WL*	PDM –F A/T/WL	Academic	Academic
2				
3	Academic	Academic		
4				
5			PDM – FA/T/WL	PDM – FA/T/WL
6				

Academic Teams for Grades A and B have preparation time during Periods 1 and 2. Academic Teams for Grades C and D have preparation time during Periods 5 and 6. PDM and FA/T/WL Teams have preparation time during Periods 3 and 4.
* PDM = Personal Decision-Making, FA = Fine Arts, T = Technology, WL = World Languages

Periods	Grade A	Grade B	Grade C	Grade D
1	Academic	Academic	Academic	Academic
2				
3	PDM –FA /T/WL	PDM – FA/T/WL		
4				
5	Academic	Academic	PDM-FA/T/WL	PDM –FA/T/WL
6				

Academic Teams for Grades A and B have preparation time during Periods 3 and 4. Academic Teams for Grades C and D have preparation time during Periods 5 and 6. PDM and FA/T/WL Teams have preparation time during Periods 1 and 2.

Periods	Grade A	Grade B	Grade C	Grade D
1	PDM –F A/T/WL	PDM – FA/T/WL	Academic	Academic
2				
3	Academic	Academic	PDM – FA/T/WL	PDM - FA/T/WL
4				
5			Academic	Academic
6				

Academic Teams for Grade A and B have preparation time during Periods 1 and 2. Academic Teams for Grades C and D have preparation time during Periods 3 and 4. PDM and FA/T/WL Teams have preparation time during Periods 5 and 6.

For the Academic Teams, the average size of instructional groups will be 22.2, 200 students divided by nine teachers. The Personal Decision-Making and Fine Arts/ Technology/World Language teams are responsible for students from two grades during each of the two-hour blocks assigned to them. The average size of an instructional group in *each* of their two-hour blocks of time will be 23.5, 400 students divided by 17 teachers.

Interdisciplinary teaching teams implement the practices of *flexible scheduling* and *flexible grouping*. Initially, the principal will play a significant role in helping teams to establish their schedules. In the long term as teaching teams work together, they will use *flexible scheduling* to more effectively use the time assigned to the team. The team will learn to schedule students into groups and course activities for amounts of time appropriate to the needs of the instructional activities planned.

With four hours allocated to the Academic Team, an easy *initial* schedule could be an hour for each of the four subject areas for each student each school day. There are likely to be some days, however, when this is not true because of special activities such as field trips or other instructional activities that may take all or a large portion of the time block. Or some students may need extra time in a specific subject area, which may reduce or eliminate time for some other subject area on some days. Again, the team makes student-scheduling decisions.

There is a significant rationale for "continuous engagement" of all students in grades 1 through 12 in the subject areas included in Personal Decision-Making. Continuous engagement does not necessarily mean daily, every-other-day, or even weekly, although it could. Students should, however, be engaged regularly, at least bi weekly or monthly, with the concept of "personal decision-making" applied in each of the three subject areas of Personal Decision-Making (Health and Physical Education, Family and Consumer Science, and Guidance).

With respect to the subject areas of Fine Arts and Technology subgroups, we propose, consistent with national content standards, a "continuous engagement" philosophy for grades 1 through 12. Again, the frequency of instructional activities will not necessarily be daily, every-other-day, or even weekly. The team could set up a schedule with instructional activities for a subject area for several days in a row, or several weeks in a row and then several days or weeks without. But months, semesters, or years should not pass without engagement in each subject. The concept of "continuous engagement" is discussed in Chapter 3.

With respect to World Languages, currently second languages are usually offered only at the high school level, and then as electives rather than as required courses. There are, however, schools that offer second languages in lower grades and that require a second language of all high school students. In Chapter 3, we address the various issues of offering and scheduling second languages.

Variations – Student Groups

The illustration presented here groups students heterogeneously by *grade level*. An acceptable alternative would be to use *multi-age/grade grouping* of students. This approach to student grouping supports and accommodates the philosophy that students mature and progress at different rates, and therefore, schools should not arbitrarily group students by age. Multi-age/grade grouping also addresses the issue of small grade level enrollments; i.e., grade level enrollments well under 200. In these cases, multi-age/grade grouping can bring the number of students in the Academic Small Learning Communities closer to 200.

Variations – Number of Members on a Teaching Team

In our illustration, we chose to organize teaching teams with nine teachers. In other situations, the number of teachers could go as high as 12. We chose these numbers so that there could usually be two teachers with the same subject area expertise on the same team. The purpose is to allow collaboration on the teaching team relative to the curriculum, assessment, and instructional pedagogy for each subject area.

There is a point of view that says that nine or more people on a team are too many to effectively work together. But there is the flexibility to accommodate both (1) two or more individuals on the teaching team who have the same subject area expertise and (2) the size of the team. The teaching team and the students assigned to the team can be divided into two parts so that, in the case of Academic Teams, there are 4.5 teachers who work with 100 students. With only one special education teacher, that person would serve both "sub-teams." It is important for the "small learning community" concept and for "looping" that the four regular education teachers work with the same 100 students over multiple years. The Personal Decision-Making Team and the Fine Arts/Technology/ World Languages

Team could be divided in a similar way. The two "sub-teams" are able to work together on issues of curriculum, assessment, and instruction when necessary or appropriate because each has the same preparation time. Making this division also has the benefit of reducing the number of different students for a given teacher to work with in any given school year.

Implementing Small Learning Communities: Some Issues

It is necessary to recognize that moving to small learning communities and implementing the other practices, although "principled," may have some controversy. Teachers, principals, and other educators with whom we have discussed these possible changes have raised the issues that we list here. We list them here only to identify and recognize them as issues. Later, in Chapters 3 and 5, we deal with them more specifically as part of the discussion of curriculum, leadership, and implementation.

Music Education – Music teachers, particularly high school instrumental music teachers, have traditionally taught their students daily, and often have less time scheduled with students than other teachers. The students are usually scheduled in larger groups and tend to be musically talented. Sometimes music teachers provide individual or group music lessons during the school day. Parents of these students are usually very interested in developing the musical talents of their children. How can music programs be organized and structured under the concept of small learning community that will achieve results equal to or greater than the results of the traditional music program?

World Languages – The teaching of World Languages, second languages to English-speaking students, has traditionally followed an "everyday" pattern for a full school year. In high schools where a "four-period day" block schedule has been implemented, this pattern has usually been modified to two quarters during the school year, not necessarily consecutive. In the small learning community, with the type of schedule proposed here, how can instruction for a second language be effectively structured to meet the goals of the second language offerings?

Teaching Role of Counselors – Counselors are not typically found in elementary schools. In middle and high schools, counselors spend much of their time dealing with individual student problems (crisis counseling) and with various administrative functions, scheduling students being prominent among them. What is required to make a change in the counsel's role to increase the time spent with groups of students teaching the Guidance curriculum? What is required to include counselors on the faculty of elementary schools where they are not already present?

Teaching Role of Library/Media Specialists – Library/media specialists are not always present on the faculty, particularly in elementary schools. Although library/media specialists typically do some group teaching of students, they have not played that role to the extent intended in the small learning community. What is required to make a change in the library/media specialist role and ensure the presence of a library/media specialist on the faculty of all schools?

Teaching Role of School Nurses – School nurses are typically not present in all schools on a full-time basis, and their group work with students is usually minimal. What is required to ensure the presence of a school nurse as a fulltime member of the faculty of all schools and establish the teaching role for school nurses envisioned in this application of the practice of small learning community?

Role of the Principal – Principals, as we have observed them, do not spend much time giving direction and support to teaching teams. In fact, teaching teams do not exist in most schools. What training and support do principals need to lead a school that is made up of small learning communities? How will principals be able to lead teacher collaboration and the practices of curriculum, assessment, and instruction advocated in this book and other educational literature?

Chapter 1: Summary and Concluding Remarks

In this chapter, we have described nine practices that a school might choose to implement. These practices are supported by research and advocated by prominent educational organizations and experts who believe they will lead to increased student achievement. These practices are implemented at the school level by the principal, but they require district level support and encouragement.

Implementing these school level instructional practices requires a different organization for teachers and students and a different structure for time in the school day than are currently found in most schools. Once the organization and structure are redesigned, the doors open to other important instructional, curricular, and assessment practices that enhance student achievement. These are the topics of Chapters 2, 3, and 4.

The nine practices are critical, and efforts should be made to implement as many of them as quickly as possible (Cotton, 2004; Cawelti, 1997). The practices and concepts described in this chapter are very closely related. Implementing **small learning communities** that are **schools-within-a-school** with teachers forming **interdisciplinary teaching teams** with responsibility for all students at a grade level (**heterogeneous groups of students**) requires establishing a school schedule that allows **common preparation time** for the teaching teams each day. Establishing the related concepts of **teacher leadership (distributed/shared leadership)** and **autonomy (distributed/ shared decision-making)** for instructional decisions enhances and strengthens teamwork but will require appropriate policies and teacher training. **Common preparation time** will facilitate teacher learning of necessary knowledge, skills, and attitudes and is an essential ingredient for effective teacher collaboration. **Differentiated staffing** for teaching teams may require policy changes, and, although desirable, could be postponed. **Looping** is a practice having sound rationale, but a decision regarding it may be postponed until at least a year after initial implementation of small learning communities.

Small learning communities with all of the attributes described in the practices discussed in this chapter are not the ends in themselves. They are enablers. They open the doors to teacher collaboration for the processes of planning, development, implementation, and evaluation for the purpose of improving instruction, curriculum, assessment, and professional practice. In Chapters 2, 3, and 4, practices related to increased student achievement for the design elements of instruction implemented by teachers, curriculum, and assessment, respectively, are discussed.

Questions for Consideration

1. To what extent is each of the school level instructional practices being implemented in the school in which you work, or one with which you are familiar?

2. What would the organization of teachers, students, and time to support small learning communities look like in the school in which you work, or one with which you are familiar?

Chapter 2 – Teacher Collaboration and Personalizing Education

> From the beginning, time must be set aside for faculty to meet regularly, converse about students and inquire, problem solve, learn, and grow their pedagogy thoughtfully and critically together.
>
> (Ancess , 1997, as cited in Cotton, 2004, p. 28)

In this chapter, we introduce instructional practices that are implemented at the teaching team level within the school; that is, teachers working in interdisciplinary teams take primary responsibility for implementing them. Researchers and prominent educational organizations and experts support the conclusion that these teacher level practices will lead to increased student achievement. Each practice will be discussed individually by giving definitions and principles and briefly describing the intended application. Because the practices are not mutually exclusive, the discussion of a specific practice may include mention of another.

The practices implemented by teachers are quality characteristics that define how the educational business of the school is to be conducted. They are:

1. Teacher collaboration,
2. Continuous professional development,
3. Personalized learning plans for teachers,
4. Flexible scheduling/grouping,
5. Personalizing students' programs,
6. Personalized plans for progress for students,
7. Personal adult advocates for students, and
8. Family involvement.

Interdisciplinary teaching teams *collaborating* with respect to instruction, curriculum, assessment, and professional growth is the central instructional practice at the teacher level. Other practices are supported and enhanced by the power of teachers working together to help students learn.

At the teaching level, the instructional practices focus on the teaching team, its individual members, time in the school day, and the students assigned to the team. This focus includes (1) how the team organizes and schedules the time it has with students, (2) how the team groups students, (3) strategies for developing relationships with students, (4) decision-making related to teaching pedagogy, strategies, and resources the team uses, and (5) the training and development of the team and its individual members. These practices are greatly enhanced by implementing teacher collaboration.

There are important teacher level instructional practices beyond those emphasized in this book. For example, this book does not consider classroom management strategies and teaching pedagogy related to specific subject areas. The instructional practices to which this book is directed are those that organize teachers, students, and time in the school day and describe ways to create more personal relationships among and between teachers and students. These practices provide *opportunity* for increasing the quality of other specific teaching practices that are part of the overall improvement strategy.

Instructional Practices
Implemented by Teachers Working in Teams

Teacher Collaboration

Definition and Principles

Collaboration occurs when a group works together, especially for intellectual purposes. Collaboration is an *opportunity* to enhance the results of problem-solving activities. As Schmoker (1999) has pointed out, "Effective collaboration is really action research--

carefully conducted experimentation with new procedures and assessment of them" (p. 16). This type of collaborative work is critical to school improvement.

As the teaching environment has become more complex, increases are needed in the breadth of knowledge and expertise of teachers. It is difficult for one teacher alone to deal with that complexity. Little notes that the complex tasks of teaching "cannot be accomplished by even the most knowledgeable individuals working alone" (as cited in Schmoker, 1999, p. 12). Little goes on to report strong relationships between effective collaboration and the improvement of both teachers and students:

- Gains in student achievement.
- Higher quality solutions to problems.
- Increased confidence among all.
- Teachers' ability to support each other's strengths and to accommodate their weaknesses.
- Teachers' ability to examine and test new ideas, methods, and materials.
- Improved assistance to beginning teachers.
- Larger pool of ideas, materials, and methods. (as cited in Schmoker, 1999, p. 12)

Marzano (2003) identifies collegiality and professionalism as school level factors that have been associated with school improvement. He highlights Villani's description of collegial behavior as demonstrated by teachers who are supportive of one another, openly enjoy professional interactions, and are respectful and courteous to each others needs (as cited in Marzano, 2003). Fullan and Hargreaves point out that collegiality doesn't work if it is "contrived." "According to Fullan and Hargreaves, [effective collegial] behaviors include

- Openly sharing failures and mistakes,
- Demonstrating respect for each other, and
- Constructively analyzing and criticizing practices and procedures. (Marzano, 2003, p. 61).

Application of *Teacher Collaboration*

Teacher collaboration in a collegial atmosphere is central to the effectiveness of small learning communities and interdisciplinary teaching teams. Teacher collaboration uses the processes of planning, development, implementation, and evaluation for the purpose of improving instruction, curriculum, assessment, and professional practice. It is through focused collaboration in teaching teams that more effective teaching practices are planned and successfully implemented. Continuous improvement of instruction, curriculum, assessment, and professional practice becomes part of the routine and culture of the teaching teams and, therefore, part of the routine and culture of the school. School improvement *happens* at the teaching team level.

Interdisciplinary teaching teams have an *opportunity* to meet and work together collaboratively for one third of each school day (two hours in a six hour student school day). Teacher collaboration, however, will not just happen. The principal must provide the teaching and coaching that teams need to build the skills and attitudes teachers need for effective collaboration. In many cases, perhaps most, provisions for training principals for this critical role and task will be necessary. Early in the implementation, the principal will provide a relatively high degree of leadership through training and coaching. During this early time as a team, the members must learn to work together focusing on (1) the team's collective responsibility for providing instruction that meets the needs of all students in the small learning community, (2) instruction that is aligned with the curriculum that establishes the team's collective goals, and (3) the assessment programs that measure each student's progress and achievement with respect to those goals. At the beginning, the principal must model the structuring of meeting time and facilitate/lead meeting activities. In this way the principal enhances collaborative and leadership skills of team members and demonstrates expectations for the use of collaborative work time and the processes involved.

Note that the two hours per school day of common preparation time for the teaching teams also includes preparation time for individual teachers and for subgroups that may be working on projects together. Also, note that the expanded time during the school day is not a substitute for time that is currently available before and after school and outside of the school day and the school year.

Continuous Professional Development

Definition and Principles

Effective adult learning on-the-job in schools should be (1) a continuous process, (2) personalized to the needs of the individual, (3) based on needs derived from curriculum, assessment, instruction, and student issues, and (4) include opportunities for learning, with guided practice and feedback, on-the-job (job-embedded) and outside of the work environment. Cotton (2004) reports, "Most of these [small] schools design their own professional development, which is focused on how to work more effectively with students" (p. 28). *Breaking Ranks II*™ (NASSP, 2004) describes important qualities of professional development: "Ensure that professional development is continuous and that each development opportunity is reinforced with follow-up activities" (p. 14).

Continuous professional development suggests that learning on the part of teachers never ends. At times, needed learning will be relatively simple and require a short amount of time and a small amount of effort. At other times, the magnitude and effort will be considerable, but the nature of the work of teaching and the problems encountered in the process require that teachers be open to learning new knowledge and skills all the time. Some professional development challenges result from shortcomings of pre-service training, or the simple fact that the knowledge and skills taught in pre-service teacher training are not fully developed and require continued practice with feedback. Other learning challenges come from new curriculum, new instructional methods and materials, new requirements with respect to assessment and the use of assessment data, new information technology, increased performance standards for schools, accountability, and accommodating students with learning problems.

Application of *Continuous Professional Development*

Each team will have control over most of its professional development. The exceptions are related to district-wide curriculum and assessment practices that will be described in Chapters 3 and 4, and school-wide practices already described in Chapter 1. For example, the school must provide and require teacher participation in professional development for the knowledge, skills, and attitudes necessary for successful teacher collaboration. The district must also require professional development for its curriculum and assessment policies.

The team will identify its needs based on the competencies that need to be developed; i.e., competencies that are not present in team members in sufficient quantity or quality to implement new practices and to achieve the expected student-learning results. The team will assess the need for new and/or improved competencies. Sometimes competencies are not required of the entire team. Then, we suggest delegation of the development to team members according to current strengths, weaknesses, and interests. Ad hoc partnerships between team members may be created to provide coaching, mentoring, feedback, and support. The teaching team will decide how to allocate time and dollar resources to the team's professional development according to the team's needs as identified in its planning, development, implementation, and evaluation activities.

Personal Learning Plans (for teachers)

Definition and Principles

Personal Learning Plans for teachers identify specific learning objectives along with strategies and action plans for achieving the learning objectives. They are focused on the learning needs that arise from action plans for strategies designed to implement and improve instruction, curriculum, assessment, and professional practice. These plans "take into account the skills and knowledge each staff member must acquire to implement the action plan" (NASSP, 2004, p. 34). These plans work toward implementing the instructional, curricular, and assessment practices.

Application of *Personal Learning Plans (for teachers)*

Each member of the team creates a Personal Learning Plan. In the redesigned school envisioned here, the Personal Learning Plan for teachers is embedded in The One Page® Plan that each teacher writes as part of the school's planning process. (See Chapter 5 and Appendix D for details of The One Page® Plan format, contents, and methodology.) These plans include personal vision and mission with respect to the teacher's assignment, measurable objectives for student learning, strategies for achieving the objectives, and action plans for implementing the strategies. The Personal Learning Plan results from a teacher's professional development needs with respect to the strategies and action plans for achieving the objectives for student learning. The teacher's plan will be "fluid" and subject to modification during the school year as instructional, curricular, and assessment issues and problems arise that must be solved.

Flexible Scheduling/Grouping

Definition and Principles

School schedules are flexible to the extent that time and the size of student instructional/learning groups vary. The grouping of students can also be flexible based on the needs of students at any given time. Instructional activities should vary depending on the appropriate amount of time necessary, the appropriate group size, and the specific students that need to be involved. Therefore, variations take into account the type and purpose of the instructional activity that is to take place as well as the instructional needs of students; e.g., remedial instruction. When time and group sizes are varied according to the type and purpose of the instructional activity, the probability of successful learning for individual students increases.

Application *Flexible Scheduling/Grouping*

In the late 1960s and 1970s, flexible scheduling of schools became quite popular. Based on the ideas of Trump and Baynham (1961), Bush and Allen (1964), and Trump (1977) many high schools and middle/junior high schools used flexible scheduling. New school facilities were designed and built to accommodate large and small group instruction. But this type of scheduling became less "fashionable" and was dropped in most of the schools that had implemented it. More recently, "block scheduling" which features larger blocks of time; e.g., four 90-minute periods per day; and the "four period day" have been implemented in many high schools. This scheme allows individual teachers greater flexibility in structuring and scheduling different instructional activities within the longer class periods. In some cases, teachers have created teams and combined their students to integrate curriculum.

In the redesigned school envisioned in this book, flexible scheduling/grouping does not take place at the school level. Rather flexible scheduling/grouping is done at the teaching team level providing the opportunity for teaching teams to vary time and the size and make-up of student groups whenever the team sees the need. The teaching teams make their own decisions about the use of the time allocated to them and the grouping and regrouping of students.

Personalizing Students' Programs

Definition and Principles

Clarke defines personalization as

> A learning process in which students receive close support of adult mentors and guides to assess their own talents and aspirations, plan a pathway toward their own purposes, work cooperatively with others on challenging tasks, maintain a record of their explorations, and demonstrate their learning against clear standards in a wide

56

variety of media, all with the close support of adult mentors and guides (as cited in NASSP 2004, p. 67).

For personalization, Keefe and Jenkins (2002) emphasize the importance of taking into account individual student characteristics and needs; such as learning styles, learning skills, past performance, talents, and interests; and making use of the concept of differentiated instruction. Teachers who personalize the learning experiences for students help students to diagnose cognitive strengths and weaknesses and to develop Personal Plans for Progress. They adapt instruction to learner needs and interests and mentor authentic and reflective learning experiences for students. Personalizing with respect to student interests leads to student engagement in instruction (NASSP, 2004). When Tomlison and Allen (2000) discuss differentiation of instruction, they note the importance of flexible grouping; ongoing assessment; differentiation of content, process, and product; and consideration of students' readiness, interests, and learning profiles.

In *Breaking Ranks II™*, NASSP (2004) notes the importance of personalization for strengthened relationships among students, teachers, staff members, and families. Cotton (2002) in a discussion of the importance of "knowing students well" states: "When teachers and students are able to build relationships, both are motivated to work and to make a success of the schooling enterprise" (pp. 23-24). Teachers in small learning communities, according to Cotton (2004), are able to become more knowledgeable about student strengths and needs and to respond to them more effectively than in larger educational environments.

Application of *Personalizing Students' Programs*

The practices associated with small learning communities support the building of meaningful relationships among the people included in each small learning community: teachers, students, families, and other staff members on the teaching team. In a redesigned school, teachers working in interdisciplinary teams implement the six elements of personalized instruction proposed by Jenkins and Keefe (2002):

1. A dual teacher role of coach and advisor (personal advocate for each student);
2. The diagnosis of relevant student learning characteristics (personalization);
3. A collegial school culture (collaboration);
4. An interactive learning environment;
5. Flexible scheduling and pacing (personalization); and
6. Authentic assessment.

Teaching teams will complete an assessment of students that includes learning styles, past performance, and student strengths and interests. This diagnosis will guide the planning of each student's educational program and the prescription of instructional activities (Personal Plans for Progress). Teachers will vary instructional strategies based on what they have learned about students' characteristics.

Personal Plan for Progress (for students)

Definition and Principles

A student's educational/learning plan is personalized when the plan takes into account important characteristics of the individual that are relevant to the purpose of the plan. Therefore, a personalized plan has a higher probability of achieving its goals. Important to the concept of a Personalized Plan for Progress is the inclusion of the student's "reflections on personal aspirations and an academic courses plan and school activities strategy that may lead to realization of those aspirations" (NASSP, 2004, p. 10). Keefe and Jenkins (2002) advocate the use of developmental characteristics, student learning styles (including cognitive, affective, and physiological styles), and student learning history.

An important issue for personal education plans for all students is one of information management. We need to consider *more* individual characteristics of students, using that information to prescribe instruction and assessment on a *more* individual basis. The teaching team needs systems and processes to collect information and to use that information to personalize instruction. The Personal Adult Advocate for the student needs to help the student manage the information.

Application of *Personal Plans for Progress*

In schools today, each student has an educational plan. The goal of the Personalized Plan for Progress is to make the plan *more* personalized and individualized. Currently, for any given school year, a student's educational plan consists of (1) the courses in which the student is enrolled for the year, (2) the teacher or teachers to whom the student is assigned along with the methods and materials the teachers use, and (3) the assessments that are used to measure the student's learning. As students progress through the grades, their plans tend to become more personalized with respect to goals because students have some choices (electives) with respect to courses. Teachers are able to provide some personalization of instruction by giving individual or group help during class periods, before school, or after school. Assessments are much the same for all students, exceptions being projects in which students may have some choices about specific topics or options for the presentation format. Special education students who may have modified assessments are also exceptions.

The intention in a redesigned school is for every student to have a Personal Plan for Progress. The plan's development is a joint responsibility of the Personal Adult Advocate, the student, and the student's parents, but the student writes the plan. As students progress through the grades, it is expected that they will take increasingly more responsibility for their plans. They will demonstrate greater independence in the development of the plan and in the implementation and evaluation of the results.

The Personal Plan for Progress is intended to provide students with an opportunity to look to *their* future as they would like it to be (their aspirations) and to identify the objectives, strategies, and action plans that will help them to realize their visions. In the planning process, descriptions of student characteristics, such as learning style, learning history, talents, interests, strengths, and weaknesses, will be used to establish vision, mission, objectives, strategies, and action plans.

Personal Adult Advocate

Definition and Principles

The concept of a Personal Adult Advocate is one that is similar to the popular notion of "personal coach." The student has an adult in the school who not only advocates for the student's needs, but also provides guidance and accountability as the student pursues his or her goals. Even the most competent people benefit from advocates and coaches.

A major purpose of the Personal Adult Advocate is to ensure that each student is well known by at least one adult in the school. This adult will create a personal relationship with the student (Cotton, 2004). This relationship can be a significant motivator for students.

Application of *Personal Adult Advocate*

The practice of Personal Adult Advocate is applied by ensuring that each student has at least one teacher who has a personal relationship with the student so that the student will (1) receive guidance for establishing goals, (2) set a clear path toward goal achievement, and (3) be held accountable for making progress. Through implementation of the small learning community concept and teaching teams with looping, a mechanism is established to match students with teachers appropriately and to create opportunities for the teacher/advocate and the student to build a long-term relationship with qualities of trust and openness. The number of students assigned to one teacher advocate will depend on the student-to-teacher ratio in the school.

The Academic Team will assign each student to one teacher member of the team. That teacher will build a relationship with each assigned student and his or her family over several years, up to four (because of looping). Special education teachers will usually become the Personal Adult Advocate for special education students. The number of students per Academic Personal Adult Advocate will be 20 to 30 depending upon the student-to teacher ratio in the school.

The Personal Decision-Making Team also uses the concept of Personal Adult Advocate to establish teacher advocate relationships with students, although the number of students assigned to a teacher advocate will usually exceed 30. Therefore, students will have at least two Personal Adult Advocates. This will be particularly meaningful and important for the Personal Decision-Making Team. Providing guidance and accountability related to objectives, strategies, and action plans for health and fitness, educational and career planning, appropriate behavior, and issues such as social and emotional competence are critical to future effectiveness of the student. The nature of the curriculum for Personal Decision-Making makes the practice of Personal Adult Advocate particularly meaningful.

With respect to the Fine Arts/Technology/World Languages Team, students may have a third Personal Adult Advocate. In the cases of students who have special talents and interests in the Fine Arts, Technology, or a second language, a Personal Adult Advocate can be very meaningful.

Family Involvement

Definition and Principles

Family involvement implies that the members of the student's family, particularly parents, but also siblings and extended family, are partners in the education of the student. Family participation in the teaching and learning of students can enhance motivation and achievement. Family involvement also includes the participation of parents on a regular basis as volunteer members of the teaching team and as volunteers on an ad hoc basis to contribute special knowledge and skills. According to Cawelti (1997), "parent involvement activities include offering training in parenting skills, providing learning activities for parents to help with at home, enlisting volunteers, and improving communication through effective conferences and other information-providing activities" (p. 19).

Application of *Family Involvement*

Teaching teams encourage and welcome parent participation. This role includes (1) participation in decision-making related to the development of the student's Personal Plan for Progress; (2) participation, support, and supervision of the implementation of the Personal Plan for Progress outside of the school and school day; (3) monitoring the student's progress; and (4) communicating with the school and teaching team. Instruction is designed to include student work outside of school that enables parents to participate, supervise, and monitor students' activities and learning results.

Teaching teams recruit and train parent volunteers to work with team members during the school day. Volunteer work includes both working with teachers during instructional activities and working with support staff; e.g., instructional aides; to support the work of teachers. All volunteers work under the direction of teachers and within the policies and regulations set by the district and school for volunteers.

Chapter 2: Summary and Concluding Remarks

The implementation of the school level instructional practices described in Chapter 1 enables the implementation of practices implemented by teachers working in teams. In Chapter 1, the creation of small learning communities that are interdisciplinary teaching teams working with specific groups of students over multiple years was discussed. That organizational structure provides the *opportunity* for (1) effective, sustainable implementation of teacher collaboration, (2) continuous and personalized professional development for teachers and other staff, and (3) more personalized and individualized teaching practices which guarantee that each student will be known well by school personnel and be engaged in instruction.

62

Questions for Consideration

1. What is the nature of teacher collaboration in your school?

2. How are the processes of planning, development, implementation, and evaluation, built into teacher collaboration? Or, how could they be?

3. To what extent is teacher collaboration focused on instruction, curriculum, assessment, and professional growth in your school?

4. What additional efforts could be made to increase personalization for students in your school?

5. In what ways are families involved in the education of students in your school? What additional ways would be helpful?

Chapter 3 – Curriculum Redesign

Begin with the end in mind.

(Covey, 1989)

In this chapter, we begin by defining curriculum as a description of the learning results that the school and teachers are attempting to achieve with students. This is followed by a brief discussion of leadership for curriculum. We then present curriculum practices. Finally, we discuss the rationale for the subject area groupings used to form interdisciplinary teaching teams and special issues of the assignment of counselors, school nurses, and library/media specialists to teaching teams.

What is Curriculum?

Curriculum has many definitions. Cuban states: "Over 1,100 curriculum books have been written since the turn of the [20ᵗʰ] century, each with a different version of what 'curriculum' means" (as cited in Marzano, 2003, p. 106). These definitions often refer to "experiences" which students have under the direction of the teacher or school. Such definitions of curriculum overlap with teaching and instruction. In this book, we have chosen to clearly distinguish between curriculum and instruction, with curriculum describing the educational "ends" and instruction describing the educational "means." Therefore, we define curriculum as a description of the *learning results* that the school and teachers are attempting to achieve through instruction.

Leaders' Responsibility for Curriculum

Marzano et al. (2005) in their meta-analysis study of school leadership practices of principals found that among the 21 school leadership responsibilities that correlated positively and significantly with student achievement were *knowledge* of current curriculum practices and *involvement* in the design and implementation of curriculum. Although it may be necessary, and it is appropriate, for the principal to delegate *some* of these leadership responsibilities to other school level leaders, the principal must be both knowledgeable and involved in some curriculum design and implementation.

Leaders at the district level also have responsibility for curriculum. Their role is considered in the discussion of curriculum practices later in this chapter. Briefly, curriculum leaders at the district level have a responsibility to establish a common curriculum framework that will be used throughout the district, ensure that learning expectations are the same in all schools, and facilitate the writing of the curriculum documents.

Curriculum Design

We have selected eight curriculum practices for emphasis when redesigning schools. Six are taken directly from the five major sources for practices we have used; two are included based on the authors' experience and philosophy. These curriculum practices are the focus of curriculum development efforts in the school and in the district. They are:

1. Curriculum framework (included by the authors),
2. Curriculum development,
3. Curriculum alignment with content standards,
4. Clearly stated vision and mission focused on student learning,
5. Essential learnings and high expectations,
6. Career focus in all courses,
7. Continuous engagement in all subject areas (included by the authors), and
8. Curriculum integration.

The discussion of curriculum practices includes "definitions and principles" and the "intended applications." There is overlap among the practices. This overlap is seen when one practice is used in the definition or description of another.

Curriculum Framework

Definition and Principles

A curriculum framework identifies the content and format of curriculum documents along with the technical writing rules used to create the various components. There is not just one useful curriculum framework. There are, however, two important principles that should guide the selection and use of a curriculum framework:

1. The framework should provide enough detail to effectively guide teachers in the development of instruction and assessment. Without sufficient detail, alignment of instruction and assessment with curriculum will be problematic.
2. The framework should be used for all subject areas at all grade levels. This provides common language and understanding of the framework and its application.

The curriculum framework is a communication tool that begins with general (and relatively brief) descriptions of the learning results expected of students and becomes progressively more detailed. Because the curriculum framework should be common across all subject areas and grade levels, the responsibility for adopting a district-wide curriculum framework lies with district leaders.

Application of a *Curriculum Framework*

As an example of a curriculum framework, we present one that we have found to be useful and that meets the two criteria given above. The framework components are shown in Figure 3-1.

Figure 3-1. Curriculum Framework - Components

Subject Area	
Philosophy:	A brief presentation of the expected learning results of a subject area and why the results are important
Strands:	Titles of major themes in the subject area along with brief descriptions
Programs Goals:	Statements that describe in general terms what students are to learn within each strand
Scope Outline:	An outline showing skills and concepts and sub-skills and sub-concepts for each program goal
Scope and Sequence Grid:	A matrix of skills and concepts that shows their grade-level/course placement and identifies the level of learning at each grade level
Learner Outcomes:	Statements which include (1) only one expected behavior (only one verb) at the appropriate level of learning taxonomy (cognitive*, psychomotor, or affective), (2) the criteria for successful learning, and (3) the conditions under which the student will learn and be assessed

*Tom Gusky (2005) suggests use of a cognitive taxonomy similar to Bloom's (1956) to establish clarity with regard to what students should learn (knowledge) and what they should be able to do with what they have learned (translation, application, analysis, and synthesis).

It is beyond the scope of this book to deal with the technical writing formats and rules for the components of the framework. Examples of useful taxonomies of learner outcomes (objectives) would be Bloom (1956) for the cognitive domain, Simpson (1972) for the psychomotor domain, and Krathlwohl et al. (1964) for the affective domain.

Learner outcomes in the affective domain are frequently omitted from the school's written curriculum. However, we agree with Popham (2005) that "student attitudes count" (p. 84). Developing positive attitudes toward school, learning, and important aspects of our culture and society are critical learning results that should be part of the school's curriculum that are systematically taught and measured.

Curriculum Development

Definition and Principles

Curriculum development is the application of the curriculum framework to the writing of curriculum documents. This is an iterative, technical writing process. It begins with a pre-writing review of state and national content standards and trends and issues related to the subject area. Then each component of the framework is drafted applying the technical writing rules for the component, revised, and edited based on feedback from reviewers. As progress with writing is made through the components of the framework, previous components are subject to revision.

Curriculum development is critical to student achievement. Curriculum development is the process used to implement the important practice of establishing *essential learnings and high expectations* in *all* subject areas for *all* students (NASSP, 2004).

Application of *Curriculum Development*

Historically, schools have been unable to adequately support and carry out the tasks of curriculum development. When budgets are tight, as is usually the case in school districts, *development* of any kind is an easy target for reductions or eliminations needed to balance the budget. Effective curriculum development is also problematic because the knowledge and skill for doing it tends to be centralized in a few people at the district office in larger districts and may be missing completely in smaller districts. In addition, curriculum development has not been a high priority in teacher or administrator preparation. The result is that teachers, who need to do much of the work of curriculum development, and principals, who need to have knowledge and involvement in curriculum development, are often not well prepared for this important task. How can the shortage of knowledge and resources for curriculum development be overcome? A *redesign* of the organization and structure is needed.

68

First, by redesigning the organization of teachers and the structure of time in the school day to increase the amount of collaborative time available to teaching teams, the time resource for curriculum development, as well as needed professional development, can be significantly increased and focused. This is the redesign that was described in Chapter 1. Second, curriculum development can be simplified (but not made simple) by adopting a curriculum framework that is used for *all* subject areas and across *all* grade levels. Third, writing the first five components of the curriculum framework just described in Figure 3-1 can be done in a relatively short period of time using national or state content standards as guides. This effort is a district responsibility. The district must provide leadership and coordination that involves teachers who do the writing. Professional development of *all* teachers and principals is required to ensure understanding of the framework and the capacity of *all* teachers and *all* principals to apply it to the writing of curriculum documents.

There are time and dollar resources applied to curriculum development in schools today. Whatever resources are currently applied need to be continued. These resources usually provide for time outside the school day or school year or provide substitute teachers during the school day. This time resource and a part of the increased preparation time during the school day must be clearly focused on the curriculum development task through professional development of teachers, a common curriculum framework, and curriculum leadership at the district and school levels.

District level curriculum leaders coordinate and facilitate the development of the curriculum for each subject area. This collaboration within a *subject area department* is important so that there is consistency of learning expectations among all students taking a course. District level curriculum leaders take specific responsibility for working face-to-face with teacher committees from each subject area to write the first five components of the framework (Philosophy, Strands, Program Goals, Scope Outline, and Scope and Sequence Grid). In small school districts where the number of district leaders is small, several school districts working together and/or the use of consultants can help to "shoulder the load." But a district leader, perhaps the superintendent, must be actively involved.

Note that the Scope and Sequence Grid provides for the important application of *curriculum articulation* in the curriculum development process. This ensures that skills and concepts will be logically sequenced, prevents gaps in the learning sequence, and prevents unnecessary duplication.

Approaches to writing learner outcomes, the most complicated and time-consuming part of curriculum development, may vary. One approach is for learner outcomes to be written by a committee of teachers (and leaders) as part of, and at the same time as, the writing of the first five components of the curriculum framework. With this approach, teachers will, during the school year, create units of instruction by selecting learner outcomes that logically go together and apply them in the instructional development task.

Another approach is for each teacher to write learner outcomes as the *second* step in developing units of instruction. In this case, the *first* step in developing instructional units is to logically group skills and concepts (and/or sub-skills and sub-concepts) from the scope outline and the scope and sequence grid.

With either approach, the process requires district coordination to ensure comparability among schools. Teachers will use their committee time together and/or the district's computer network (or the Internet) to *collaborate* with other teachers and communicate with district curriculum leaders as they develop instructional units. The principal's responsibility for knowledge of, and involvement in, the design of instruction requires that the principal be engaged with the writing of learner outcomes and development of instructional units (Marzano et al., 2005). Leading teacher training, reviewing teacher work, and giving feedback can accomplish this. This is an area where the principal may delegate/distribute leadership responsibility to team leaders, but the principal should still be an active participant.

Curriculum Alignment with Content Standards

Definition and Principles

Ravitch (2006) makes, as have others, a useful distinction between *content standards*, what students are expected to learn, and *performance standards*, measures of how well students have actually learned what they were expected to learn. *Content standards* guide curriculum development, while *performance standards* have implications for assessment. Performance standards are discussed in Chapter 4.

State and national documents have been written to establish and describe the learning expectations for students from the state and national perspectives. There are no "federal" content standards, per se. The "national" content standards have been created over the last couple of decades by the national professional subject matter organizations; mathematics content standards by the National Council of Teachers of Mathematics is an early and prominent example. State content standards documents often use the national documents as a base. Mark Musick, chairman of the National Assessment Governing Board, has contended that content standards are very similar across the states (as cited in Ravitch, 2006). It is performance standards that vary greatly from state to state (Ravitch, 2006).

National and state content standards documents do not equal curriculum. They do not meet the important criteria for a curriculum framework. They do not provide enough detail to guide teachers in the development of instruction and assessment, and they do not provide a common framework for all subject areas. Teachers must work with content standards documents to extend them to create a curriculum for each subject area. Reeves (2005b) states: "Schools and school systems must translate standards into a set of rational, relevant, and above all *focused* expectations" (p. 46). Figure 3-2 illustrates the sequence of the alignment of development tasks.

Figure 3-2. Alignment of Development Tasks

At this time, national and state mandates for content standards may not deal with all subject areas. They focus on the Academic Subject Areas. But content standards are important in *all* subject areas. Trump (1977) in his discussion of basic curriculum needs for "the school for everyone," suggested that there should be "no favorites" among subject areas: "No area is more essential than the others" (p. 84). Establishing content standards in a subject area communicates its importance. Schools use time and dollar resources to offer many courses in subject areas beyond the Academic Subject Areas. To get the most benefit from the time and dollar investment, *all* subject areas should have curriculum documents that align with content standards and should have performance standards.

Application of *Curriculum Alignment with Content Standards*

Our experience suggests that most school curriculum is not well aligned with state or national content standards because of the problems identified in the discussion of curriculum development; the lack of knowledge of, and the time and leadership for, curriculum development. By redesigning the organization for teachers and the structure of time in the school day, additional time will be provided for the professional growth and curriculum development tasks needed to align a school's curriculum with state or national content standards.

Content standards exist for all subject areas. The national professional subject area organizations have written them. Therefore, schools have access to content standards for all subject areas, either from the state or from the national subject area organizations. National content standards are particularly helpful in writing the first five components of the curriculum framework: Philosophy, Strands, Program Goals, Scope Outline, and Scope and Sequence Grid. They are recommended for use when states have not established content standards for a subject area.

Clearly Stated Vision and Mission Focused on Student Learning

Definition and Principles

A *vision statement* describes an intended future state. As the word "vision" suggests, the question is: What will the *school* look like? *School* here does not refer to a building; it refers to an educational institution, the people who work in it, what they are trying to accomplish, and how. "Vision statements should be expansive and idealistic. They should stimulate thinking, communicate passion, and paint a very graphic picture of the business you want" (Horan, 2004, p. 29). Picking up on "focus on student learning," the vision must deal with success relative to student learning; that is, success relative to the learning expectations described in the curriculum documents and measured by the assessment instruments that will be described and discussed in Chapter 4. A vision statement addresses the questions of who, what, where, when, and how (Horan, 2004).

A *mission statement* addresses purpose: Why does the *school* exist? Further, the mission statement can address a school's uniqueness, how it can be distinguished from other schools, and the promises it makes to students and parents (Horan, 2004). Again, "focus on learning" requires that the mission statements relate to success relative to student learning.

Literature Support for Vision and Mission Focused on Learning
"Small-school restructuring experts insist that those starting up a new school/learning community must go through a process of creating a vision and mission that can guide and inspire those associated with it" (Cotton 2004, page 20). "Focus on mastery, not coverage; focus on what is learned, not simply what is taught" (NASSP, 2004, p. 7). "The principal will provide leadership in the high school community by building and maintaining a vision, direction, and focus for student learning" (NASSP, 2004, p. 61). A *clearly stated and focused school mission* is an important factor in student achievement identified in the effective schools research. (Taylor, 2002) Among the examples that Marzano et al. (2005) include as important for the leader responsibility of *focus* are: • "Establishing concrete goals for curriculum, instruction, and assessment practices within the school" and • "Establishing high, concrete goals, and expectations that all students will meet them" (p. 50).

Application of *Clearly Stated Vision and Mission Focused on Student Learning*

Vision and mission statements focused on learning results are clearly important to a school. In redesigning schools, it is also important for teaching teams, teachers, and students to have clearly defined vision and mission statements focused on student learning. The vision and mission statements at the district, school, teaching team, teacher, and student levels focus on learning results that are described in the curriculum. This focus answers the vision question: "What?" For the district, the focus is the entire K-12 curriculum. For the school, the focus is the entire curriculum for the grade levels in the school. For a teaching team, the focus is the entire curriculum for which the team has collective/shared responsibility for teaching and accountability for the learning results. For individual teachers, the focus is the particular subject area(s) and course(s) they teach. For students, the focus is the particular subject areas and courses in which they are enrolled. Note that the focus narrows as it moves from the district level to students, but the focus is always on the relevant learning results described in the curriculum.

Horan's (2004) definition of vision includes not only *what* but also *where, who, when, why,* and *how*. The *where* is the geographical community served by the school district and the schools' locations. The *who* are the people who work in the school, staff and students. The *when* is a period of time. Vision and mission statements are futuristic, forward looking. Therefore, the time period is multi-year. The *why* refers to reasons for pursuing the learning results.

The *how* refers to favored practices used to achieve the learning results; i.e., the *means,* instruction, used to achieve the *ends* described in the curriculum. As Marzano et al. (2005) have noted, focus is not only important relative to learning results, it is also important relative to instructional practices. To increase the achievement of learning results, instructional practices must change. But Fullan (2001) notes that change in instructional practices are not always well focused: "The main problem is not the absence of innovation in schools, but rather the presence of too many disconnected, episodic, fragmented, superficially adorned projects" (p. 2). When redesigning a school, changes in practices must be selected carefully and then pursued by leaders with clarity and tenacity over a sustained period of time. Waite, Campbell, Gau, Jacobs, Rex, and Hess (2006) describe it this way: "The magic is not in a particular program – there are many good ones. The magic occurs when the school finds a program and sticks with it" (p. 36).

Essential Learnings and High Expectations

Definition and Principles

Essential learnings are those that *all* students should master. State and national content standards include what is *essential* in the various subject areas, and these essentials should then be reflected in the curriculum developed in schools.

Essential learnings have expanded over the years with the increase of technological know-how in all fields and the growing complexity of the general social and physical global environment in which we all live and work. Therefore, expectations of all students need to be greater now than in the past. The effective schools research identified the important positive relationship between *high expectations* for all students and increasing the achievement of all students (Edmonds, 1979). *Breaking Ranks II™* (NASSP, 2004) encourages "raising the level of academic rigor in all classes" (p. 7) and finding "alternatives to tracking and ability grouping" (p. 123).

Application of *Essential Learnings and High Expectations*

In a redesigned school, essential learnings are established in state and national content standards. They are included in the written curriculum documents used in the school. Essential learnings exist in *all* subject areas. Increasingly higher expectations for essential learnings are established for *all* students. No subject areas are left out when it comes to essential learnings and high expectations. It can be easily argued that "children are being left behind" not only in the academic subjects, but also in health and physical fitness, career knowledge and selection, personal financial practices, the fine arts, technology, and world languages. A major feature of redesigning the curriculum is requiring each subject area to establish, and measure the achievement of, high expectations for *all* students.

Career Focus in All Subject Areas

Definition and Principles

All subject areas have careers related to them. If schooling is preparation for the future lives of students, then effectively relating characteristics and qualities of careers to subject areas is essential for developing students' understanding of the relationship between their skills, talents, and interests and various career fields. *Breaking Ranks II™* includes career exploration as a strategy related to connecting curriculum content to real life applications of knowledge and skills to help students link their education to their future (NASSP 2004).

Dr. Mel Levine (2005) describes the need for career focus in education: "We are in the midst of an epidemic of work-life unreadiness because an alarming number of emerging adults are unable to find a good fit between their minds and their career directions" (p. 4). A *redesigned curriculum* that includes career information and applications in *all* subject areas is needed. This inclusion begins at grade 1 and becomes increasingly sophisticated as students progress through the curriculum of the subject areas and through the grades. At the high school level, this takes the form of identifying career pathways and the specific tailoring of courses in all subject areas to career pathways. The goal is to make sure that students are able to make wise decisions in their Personal Plans for Progress, so that when they graduate from high school, they are well prepared to take the next steps with respect to careers, whether further education or entering a career with a specific job.

Continuous Engagement In All Subject Areas, Grades 1 through 12

Definition and Principles

Engagement in all subject areas from grades 1 through 12 means that students have a significant amount of instruction in each subject area during each quarter of each school year. "Significant" is at least 20 hours per quarter. An exception to this practice may be World Languages in elementary and middle schools where it is usually not offered.

For the Academic Subject Areas (Language Arts, Mathematics, Science, and Social Studies), this practice is already in place through grade 10. There is now some pressure to require these subject areas in grades 11 and 12. Moving toward career and community applications in the Academic Subject Areas in grades 11 and 12 is, we think, particularly desirable for *all* students.

For the Personal Decision-Making Subject Areas (Health/Physical Education, Family and Consumer Science, and Guidance), continuous engagement in grades 1 through 12 is particularly important. All of these subject areas involve *personal decision-making*; that is, teaching students the skills for making good decisions with regard to their health and fitness; nutrition; family; personal financial practices; and academic, career, and personal/social development. These skills become habits, life styles, and emotional competencies. For example, when making decisions about behavior in some social situations, students may need to make decisions and take appropriate action without much time to think about it. The development of such skills requires ongoing and frequent engagement and practice in simulated situations over a long period of time. The national professional organizations for these subject areas have created content standards that describe learning over the entire elementary and secondary school years.

For the Fine Arts/Technology/World Languages Subject Areas, the national professional subject area organizations have created standards that span K-12. The contributions to culture, career, and leisure time of successful learning in these subject areas are life enriching.

Application of *Continuous Engagement in All Subject Areas, Grades 1 through 12*

Redesigning the school with respect to the organization of teachers and students and the structure of the time in the school day as described in Chapter 1 creates the opportunity for continuous engagement in all subject areas. Redesigning curriculum for continuous engagement in each of the subject areas simplifies what has become an overly complex and fragmented set of curricular offerings to students. State and/or national content standards for each subject area span grades 1 through 12 (in some cases, K-12). This provides the basis for schools to develop curriculum for grades 1 through 12 and allows students to develop depth of knowledge and skill in all subject areas.

At first glance, continuous engagement in all subject areas may seem like a difficult, even impossible, challenge. Continuous engagement needs to be put into a practical perspective.

First, students *should not be* involved in nine or ten subject areas on a daily basis. The amount of time in a school day makes such a schedule imprudent and impractical. Second, students *will be* involved in the four Academic Subject Areas daily depending upon the scheduling decisions made by the Academic Team. The Academic Subject Areas have two thirds of each school day for instruction to be scheduled by the Academic Team.

Third, students need not be involved in the three Personal Decision-Making Subject Areas (Health and Physical Education, Family and Consumer Science, and Guidance) or the subject areas of Fine Arts and Technology daily, weekly, or even monthly; but neither should several months or a year or more go by without engagement in these subject areas. World Languages have some special issues that are discussed later in this chapter.

Learning to make effective personal decisions underlies each of the three subject areas of Personal Decision-Making. It is particularly important that students have the opportunity to continually develop and practice their decision-making skills across all three of these subject areas over all grade levels, but not all on the same day, or in the same week, or even in the same month. (An exception is physical activity, which needs weekly attention. Some physical activity, however, should take place outside of the school day.)

As students progress through the grades, the goal is greater independence in their decision-making and instructional activities, and therefore less school time will be needed. As students mature and become more independent, an important role for teachers is that of coach, imposing a measure of accountability for decisions students make and providing feedback. Teachers will use school time to engage students in simulated situations to maintain decision-making skills. An analogy showing the importance of this ongoing practice of decision-making is the airline pilot who practices, in a flight simulator, techniques that she or he hopes to never have to use while actually flying an airplane. Such practice, however, though critical, may be spaced further apart as students develop their skills.

With respect to Fine Arts and Technology, again it is not necessary that students be engaged in both subject areas daily, weekly, or monthly, but several months should not go by without some involvement in each. In the cases of Vocal and Instrumental Music, where skills are being built that require practice and feedback, involvement on a weekly basis, several times a week, is highly desirable and recommended. In the cases of Visual Arts, other Performing Arts, and Technology, instructional units lasting one to four weeks focusing on specific skills and projects can provide meaningful learning experiences for students. As students move through the grade levels and into high school, some may rightfully choose to be more engaged because of their interests and talents, and spend more time in the school year with some aspects of the Fine Arts or Technology curricula.

Curriculum Integration

Definition and Principles

Curriculum integration refers to developing instruction that involves content (skills and concepts, learner outcomes) from more than one subject area. When instructional units bring together complementary learning expectations from different subject areas, learning activities can take on a "real world" aspect that is more realistic, interesting, and motivating.

Application of *Curriculum Integration*

When teachers from different subject areas have an opportunity to meet and plan integrated instructional units, curriculum integration can be encouraged and happen. In secondary schools, the opportunity for such planning is usually not consistent or routine, and therefore, curriculum is not usually integrated. In elementary schools, where a single teacher is usually responsible for several subject areas, the opportunity for integration is high, but the breadth of curricular responsibility and the variation in individual expertise in different subject areas hinders curriculum integration.

Redesigning schools by changing the organization of teachers and the structure of time as described in Chapter 1 creates the opportunity for teachers with different subject area expertise to collaborate regularly for planning instructional units as well as the opportunity to coordinate teaching. The opportunity here is for continuous curriculum integration because teachers have the time together on a regular, daily, on-going basis.

Other Curriculum Design Considerations

Breaking Ranks II™ (2004) identifies a number of other important considerations for curriculum design and development. They include:

- Depth over breadth – The need to make sure that skills and concepts are taught and learned to higher levels of the taxonomies; for example, application and above in the cognitive domain.
- Curriculum articulation – The need to ensure that curriculum in each subject area progresses logically through the grade levels to new and more complex levels of skills and concepts.
- Real life experiences – The need to ensure that curriculum requires the use of situations and problems that are found in the world outside of school; practical applications.
- Service learning – The need to ensure that the curriculum includes skills and concepts that require students to participate in community-based learning activities that provide services to others.
- Critical thinking – The need to ensure that curriculum requires students to solve problems that require higher-order thinking skills.
- Problem solving – The need to ensure that curriculum requires students to solve problems of increasing difficulty and novelty.
- The Advanced Placement Program – The need to open the Advanced Placement Program to all students.
- The International Baccalaureate Program – The need to open the International Baccalaureate Program to all students.

We have chosen not to provide any further discussion of these considerations in this book. We urge leaders, district and school, to consider them and place them appropriately in their curriculum policies and planning.

Implementing Curriculum Practices

Responsibility for Content Standards

By federal and state constitutions, states are responsible for educating the young people of the nation. Therefore, the state is responsible for establishing learning expectations for all students who reside within the state. In the last decade or so, all but one state has written content standards for elementary and secondary education in at least some of the subject areas. The states have typically used as a reference content standards developed by the national subject area organizations, such as the National Council of Teachers of Mathematics and the National Council of Teachers of English. The focus of state work on content standards has been the Academic Subject Areas. Many states have not addressed the issue of standards for Health and Physical Education, Family and Consumer Sciences, Guidance, Fine Arts, Technology, and World Languages. In all these subject areas, the national organizations have written content standards. So while the states have the highest governmental responsibility for establishing content standards, professional organizations in each subject area have appropriately taken it upon themselves to write recommendations for content standards. From a school or school district point of view, they are a rich resource for content standards. State content standards are mandates. When state content standards have not been written for a subject area, the content standards of the national organizations are available to use.

The second level of governmental responsibility for educating young people is the local board of education. The local board of education is required to adopt the content standards established by the state, but it is within its authority to establish content standards that go beyond the state requirements. Therefore, local school district boards may, and should, establish content standards in all subject areas offered to students. Boards should use state mandated standards when they exist and develop their own or adopt the content standards of national subject area organizations when state standards do not exist. School boards may, if they choose, add content standards in subject areas for which state mandated content standards do exist.

School boards are also responsible for the delivery of instruction – that is, teaching. This instruction is intended to result in student learning of the content standards. Therefore, the responsibility for creating a school curriculum and instructional program lies with the boards of education as a matter of policy and with superintendents for operational implementation.

Responsibility for Curriculum

Boards of education are responsible for establishing the curriculum as policy. But, as a practical matter, teachers in school districts should, and must, play the important role of doing most of the writing work. The boards, therefore, set both directive and encouraging policies to guide the teachers' work in developing curriculum documents. To ensure district-wide consistency, writing curriculum documents needs to have district level leadership, coordination, and supervision. District-wide consistency is an important part of ensuring equal educational opportunity for all students. Teachers, with the leadership and involvement of district leaders and principals, will do the actual writing of the curriculum documents. In the end, when the curriculum documents have been written, they are recommended to the superintendent of schools, who makes a recommendation to the board regarding approval on the basis of the documents conformity to district policy.

Through policy, the board of education should address the curriculum practices described in this chapter:

1. A *curriculum framework* that describes the format, content, and technical writing rules for the district's curriculum documents,
2. *Curriculum development* process and involvement,

3. *Alignment* of the district curriculum with state, national, and local content standards,

4. *Vision and mission statements* focused on learning results,

5. Identification of *essential learnings* in all subject areas and *high expectations* for learning of all students in all subject areas,

6. *Career focus* in all subject areas at all grade levels,

7. *Continuous engagement* of all students is all subject areas in grades 1 through 12, and

8. Encouraging *curriculum integration* of subject areas represented on interdisciplinary teaching teams.

Alignment of Teaching Teams and Curriculum

In Chapter 1, we proposed organizing interdisciplinary teaching teams by creating three groups of subject areas. Figure 3-4 shows those groupings again. The intent of these groupings is to create small learning communities by grouping subject areas logically to form interdisciplinary teaching teams that would be responsible for teaching the curriculum of their subject areas to students.

Figure 3-4. Subject Areas Assigned to Teaching Teams

Academic	Personal Decision-Making	Fine Arts/Technology/ World Languages
Language Arts Mathematics Science Social Studies	Health/Physical Education Family and Consumer Sciences Guidance	Fine Arts Technology World Languages

Rationale for the Subject Area Groupings

The logic of grouping the Academic Subject Areas seems natural. They are the "basics" that include important learning skills and are the most important of all the significant subject areas. Language Arts provides necessary tools for learning and communications. Mathematics includes processes and ways of thinking that have broad and important applications in all subject areas. Science provides the background knowledge and skill for understanding and dealing with our physical environment and processes for extending our knowledge of it. Science also develops solutions for dealing with the problems created by human-environment interactions. Social Studies provides knowledge of the richness of the cultural heritage of diverse people; understanding of social, economic, and political interactions among individuals and groups; and skills to deal with conflicts among individuals and peoples. The basic skills and concepts of these subject areas interact with each other as they are applied in the daily personal, social, and work lives of people. By redesigning the school organization and structure to provide the opportunity for interdisciplinary teacher collaboration, more robust teaching resources and teaching approaches are created for instruction in these most important subject areas.

There is also clear logic in the grouping of the subject areas of Personal Decision-Making.. Each of these subject areas deals with personal decision-making that affects an individual's quality of life. Although we do not know everything about cause and effect in these areas, we do know a lot. We know a lot about the relationship between preventative measures, nutrition, and physical activity and the physical health of our bodies. Having the information and developing and applying skills of decision-making, sometimes in very difficult situations, can make the difference between injury or disease and good health. Understanding the social and psychological interactions in personal and social relationships and being able to apply decision-making skills effectively in groups – be it a work group, family, or community group – increases the potential for satisfying and productive relationships. Understanding the acquisition, accumulation, use, and stewardship of personal financial resources; of prudent consumerism; and the decision-making involved increases the potential for financial security, both short and long term. Finally, developing an individual's understanding the relationship between his or her skills, talents, and interests and the nature of careers, jobs, and work provides background for more effective career and educational decision-making. Redesigning the school structure and organization to allow integration of, and continuous student engagement with, decision-making curriculum and teaching is a more efficient and effective way of teaching the application of decision-making skills that are critical to quality of life and contribution to society.

There is one other important point to be made about the Guidance Subject Area in the Personal Decision-Making Group. Academic Development, Career Development, and Social/Personal Development include skills and concepts related to developing positive attitudes toward school, school attendance, and appropriate behavior in school. In the past, attitudes toward school have been avoided in the curriculum, and the instructional efforts relative to school attendance and behavior would be characterized more as punishment for breaking rules than as a systematic approach to teaching appropriate behavior. This is not to say that punishment is inappropriate in all cases. Rather it is to suggest that an additional, proactive instructional strategy can help to achieve the desired results. Redesigning the organization and structure of the teaching staff, students, and time provides an opportunity for a positive, preventative instructional strategy.

The relatively clear logic for the groupings of Academic Subject Areas and Personal Decision-Making Subject Areas does not hold for the Fine Arts/Technology/World Languages Subject Areas. That is why they have been divided into three subgroups that are subject areas.

The Fine Arts are made up of the Visual Arts and the Performing Arts. Visual Art is usually a static product that can be viewed. There may be motion involved and art objects can be moved into different spaces, but the product has physical boundaries in space. Examples of Visual Art include drawing, painting, sculpture, and architecture. Performing Art is performed by people for the observation and enjoyment of others. This can include viewing and/or listening. Examples of Performing Arts are singing, playing musical instruments, dancing, acting, and creative literature (short story, novel, poetry). Some individuals have and/or develop "talent" in one or more of the Fine Arts. They are the producers of the art. The purpose and the significance of Fine Arts in schools are to encourage and develop the artistic talent of these individuals. Other individuals, probably most individuals, are consumers of the Fine Arts. By developing understanding and appreciation for the Fine Arts, lives are enriched by understanding our cultural heritage and enjoying its art. Consumers of art may also be "avocational" producers of art; they produce art in their leisure time for the personal enjoyment of the artistic activity and the pleasure of completing a work of art. This, too, is life enriching. So, to encourage potential talent and to help students become good consumers of art, the Fine Arts play significant and important role in the curriculum of a school. By redesigning the organization of teachers, students, and time in the school day; by redesigning curriculum; and by introducing the practice of continuous engagement in the Fine Arts; it is possible to more effectively fulfill the purpose of the school's Fine Arts program.

Technology addresses knowledge and skills related to the use of electronic and computer-based communication, productivity, information retrieval, data processing, and problem-solving tools. This knowledge and these skills have applications across all other subject areas. Included in this subject area are the social and ethical issues of the generation and use of information. Finally, Technology includes the application of electronic technology to processes in a diverse set of industries, such as, manufacturing, health care, food, transportation, communications, etc. As students progress through the grade levels of schooling, the concepts and skills of this subject area and their applications increase in sophistication and difficulty. By grades 11 and 12, the applications relate specifically to career paths chosen by students. The redesign of school structures, organization, and curriculum to provide continuous engagement in the Technology Subject Area ensures that students have an opportunity to maximize their capacity to use electronic and computer-based technologies in their future careers.

The subject area of World Language has traditionally included languages of Spanish, French, German, and Russian. Second language offerings are being expanded in some schools to include languages of the Far East, and to some extent the Middle East. There is interest and movement toward making second language curriculum and instruction available to students below the high school level. In some school districts "language immersion" programs have been offered in elementary schools, with Spanish or French being the most popular languages. There is also some movement toward requiring a second language curriculum of all high school students. It is probably too early to call any of this a "trend," and this book is not the place to deal with the pros and cons of these issues. The redesign of schools as presented in this book, however, does provide opportunity for offering curriculum in a second language in elementary and middle level schools as well as requiring a second language of all high school students, depending on the philosophy and interest of the school or district.

Some educators feel that World Language should be included in the Academic Group. World Language teachers would probably lead the way in this regard. In fact, our early thinking had World Languages in the Academic Group. As the development of the organizational scheme unfolded, however, it became clear that more teachers were needed in the group that contained Fine Arts and Technology in order to balance teacher availability across the school day. So this compromise was made.

There are two other issues regarding World Languages that need to be mentioned. First, in most cases, second languages are still elective and offered only at the high school level. If this were to change to require second language curriculum of all students at the high school level and to include World Languages curriculum in elementary and middle level schools, expertise in World Languages would have to be added. If this expertise is to be provided by teachers physically present in the school, a shift in the distribution of teaching expertise toward World Languages would be needed in order to keep the total number of teachers at the same level. We have taken the position, which we think is a practical one, that the number of teachers cannot be increased. So, as desirable as it may be to offer second language curriculum at grade levels lower than high school and to require it of all students in high school, this is not a problem for this book to address.

Having said that, there is a way to include second language curriculum for students in elementary and middle level schools and to require second language curriculum of all high school students even though qualified teachers are not in place in the schools. As far back as the late 1950s, television has been used to introduce elementary school students to a second language. Today's computer-based instructional capabilities in schools could provide a much richer second language experience for students than television did in the past. Schools that want to adopt a philosophy of early second language curriculum, or to require second language curriculum of all high school students would have the opportunity to schedule student time with computer-based second language instruction using the organizational and structural concepts presented in Chapter 1.

It can be argued that the usual approach to teaching second languages in the high school does not align well with what we know about language learning. And indeed, our observation of the learning results of the current, usual approach is that most students do not become literate in the second language; that is, most students do not become effective communicators (speakers, listeners, readers, and writers) in the second language. A more effective approach to teaching students to become literate in a second language would include an "immersion experience," such as a summer language camp, at the beginning; and then "continuous engagement" with instruction over a long period of time, certainly longer than two school years, with a three-month summer break.

The grouping of subject areas chosen for use in this book is not perfect. It is, however, a practical compromise, which enables the implementation of the small learning communities and teacher collaboration, which are *necessary* to create the opportunity needed for the effective implementation of important instructional, curricular, and assessment practices that have great potential for increasing achievement of all students.

The Curriculum of Counselors, School Nurses, and Library/Media Specialist

We have chosen to include counselors, school nurses, and library/media specialists on interdisciplinary teaching teams with the expectation that they will be teaching their curricula to all students. The traditional role of these staff positions in schools has not included much time teaching students in groups. On the team, each is expected to bring curriculum, instruction, and assessment expertise to the team's planning, development, implementation, and evaluation processes.

Counselors

The American School Counselor Association (ASCA) has identified three "domains of student development:" Academic Development, Career Development, and Personal/Social Development (ASCA, 2005). (These "domains" are the equivalent of "strands" in the curriculum framework presented in this chapter.) Each domain has standards, competencies, and indicators. The ASCA Guidance Standards have a K-12 scope and sequence intending *continuous engagement* of students with the school's Guidance curriculum. ASCA (2005) advocates delivering the school's Guidance curriculum to students through group instruction, interdisciplinary curriculum development, and parent workshops and instruction. The redesign of schools described in this book positions the counselor on the Personal Decision-Making Team to maximize the opportunity to carry out this important teaching role for this important curriculum.

In addition to delivering the Guidance curriculum of the school, the ASCA (2005) model for a school counseling program calls for the counselor to deliver (1) *individual student planning services* through individual and small group work; (2) *responsive services* through consultation, individual and small group work, crisis counseling, referrals, and peer facilitation; and (3) *system support* including professional development, consultation, collaboration, teaming, and program management and operation. The redesign of teacher, student, and time structures in a school creates the opportunity for an effective implementation of all of the components of this model school counseling program delivery system.

School Nurses

The National Association of School Nurses (NASN) has established 16 standards for school nursing practice (NASN, 2005). The first six standards are program-related: Assessment, Diagnosis, Outcomes Identification, Planning, Implementation, and Evaluation. Although these standards rightfully emphasize an individual student's health issues and situation, the school nurse has specialized expertise in health related curriculum,

90

assessment, and instruction that enhances the breadth of knowledge available to the Personal Decision-Making Team and strengthens the collaborative approach to planning, development, implementation, and evaluation. As a member of the Personal Decision-Making Team, the school nurse will play an invaluable role in personalizing programs for individual students. The redesigned school, although not increasing the total number of teachers, does recommend that school nurses be present in every school. Some schools with very low enrollments may find this impossible. But for many schools, the presence of a fulltime school nurse will significantly increase nursing services that we recommend be applied within the Personal Decision-Making Small Learning Community.

Library/Media Specialist

The American Library Association, the Association for Educational Communications and Technology (ALA and AECT, 1998) and the International Society for Technology in Education (ISTE, 1998) have developed national standards related to Information Technology. These standards have a K-12 scope. This suggests that it is appropriate and necessary for *continuous engagement* with these standards. The library/media specialist is the key professional staff member in the school with the specialized expertise for planning, developing, implementing, and evaluating the information technology curriculum, instruction, and assessment. Knowledge and skill in the use of information technology provide students with critical communications and problem solving capabilities that can be used across all subject areas. The teaching role of the library/media specialist is key to achieving the learning expectations of the Information Technology national content standards. The redesign of schools suggested in this book, although not increasing the number of teachers, does recommend the presence of a fulltime library/media specialist in each school. In schools with very small enrollments, this may not be practical. But in many schools, the fulltime library/media specialist will provide a valuable resource that we recommend be applied to the formal teaching of the Technology subject matter to groups of students.

Chapter 3: Summary and Concluding Remarks

In this chapter, we have defined curriculum as the description of the learning results that the school and teachers are attempting to achieve through instruction. We introduced and described in terms of definition, principles, and application eight curriculum practices. We have suggested that ten subject areas be organized into three groups; Academic, Personal Decision-Making, and Fine Arts/Technology/World Languages. The purposes of the groups are (1) to establish interdisciplinary teaching teams as the teaching component of small learning communities; (2) to provide opportunity for teachers to collaborate in planning, development, implementation, and evaluation for the purpose of improving instruction, curriculum, assessment, and professional practice; and (3) to have collective/shared responsibility and accountability for the learning results of a specific group of students. The Academic Subject Areas were described as the most *important* among *significant* subject areas. But in the redesign of school structure and curriculum, all subject areas have content and performance standards and continuous engagement in the elementary and secondary school years.

Although teachers need to do most, if not all, of the work of writing the curriculum documents, curriculum leaders at the district level have the important responsibility to coordinate, facilitate, and supervise curriculum development. This coordination ensures consistency of curriculum in the district, both in terms of format and learning expectations. School principals have the critical responsibility for knowing about, and being involved in, the design and implementation of curriculum.

The membership of Academic and Personal Decision-Making teaching teams is aligned with logical groupings of subject areas. This facilitates curriculum integration among these subject areas. The subject areas of the Fine Arts/Technology/World Languages team do not share the strong logic of the other two groups. The groups were formed to meet the needs of the overall organizational scheme. These three subject areas and those that teach them, however, have the same benefits with regard to preparation time and teacher collaboration as the other two teams.

92

Finally, we discussed special issues with respect to the curriculum of some subject areas and described the support and rationale for the positions we have taken. Counselors and schools nurses have important teaching roles to play for curriculum that focuses on important personal decisions that all students make. Library/media specialists are the primary experts in most schools relative to the use of information resources in print, non-print, and electronic forms. The effective use of these information resources is basic to the education of all students.

Questions to Consider

1. What curriculum framework and development processes are used in your school? Does the framework meet the two criteria for an effective curriculum framework?

2. How are curriculum leadership functions assigned in your school and district? How well is that leadership structure working with respect to development, implementation, and supervision of curriculum?

3. To what extend is the practice of curriculum integration being applied in your school?

4. How are national and/or state content standards used to guide curriculum development in your school?

5. How well are your school's vision and mission statements focused on a future desired state of the school and student learning success?

6. What gaps are there in the instructional engagement of students in subject areas other than academic?

7. At the high school level, how can the philosophy behind the four-period day block schedule be reconciled with the concept of continuous engagement?

8. To what extent is the principal of your school knowledgeable about curriculum practices and involved in the design and implementation of the curriculum?

9. What aspects of curriculum development are included in your district's curriculum policies?

10. What is the teaching role of counselors, school nurses, and library/media specialists in your school?

Chapter 4 –Assessment Redesign

In God we trust; all others bring data.
(Maurer and Pederson, 2004, p. 33)

In this chapter we introduce six assessment practices. Four are found in the five references used as major sources for practices, and two are based on the authors' philosophy and experience. The chapter includes a definition of assessment, descriptions of the assessment practices and their intended application in a redesigned school. Finally, we describe the responsibilities for assessment development of district leaders, principals, and teachers.

What Is Assessment?

Assessment is what the school does to determine whether or not students are meeting the learning expectations that have been established in the curriculum. Assessment consists of all the measurement instruments and exercises that are used in the school to measure student accomplishment relative to the school's curriculum and progress toward meeting performance standards. Assessment also includes the systems and processes for reporting, interpreting, and using the data for purposes of reporting student progress, accountability, and improvement of instruction, curriculum, and assessment.

In addition to collecting data from measures of the learning performance of students, it is necessary to collect data regarding the instructional processes and resources used. These data relate to variables such as instructional time, instructional methodology and the quality of its application, instructional materials used, and relevant student characteristics. These data are critical to the improvement process because they create the context for the level of student performance achieved (Reeves, 2002).

Leaders' Responsibility for Assessment

Marzano et al. (2005) in their meta-analysis of school leadership practices of principals found 21 school leadership responsibilities that correlated positively and significantly with student achievement. Among them were *knowledge* of current assessment practices and *involvement* in the design and implementation of assessment practices. Although it may be necessary for the principal to delegate some of these leadership responsibilities to other school level leaders, the principal must be both knowledgeable and involved in assessment design and implementation. Leaders at the district level also have responsibility for assessment. Their role is discussed later in this chapter.

Assessment Design

The discussion of assessment practices includes definitions and principles and their intended applications. There is overlap among the practices. This overlap is seen when one practice is used in the definition or description of another.

Assessment Program

Definition and Principles

The assessment program is focused at the *course* level. (In the case of elementary school curriculum where the term "course" is not typically used, we use "course" to refer to a grade level and subject area; for example, third grade mathematics or first grade reading.) Each course has an assessment program that consists of *all* the measurement instruments and exercises used to track each student's progress and achievement through the course. The philosophy is that if the course is worth including in the school's curriculum and using school time for instruction, then the course should have an assessment program applying the same policies and principles as other courses. In other words, courses in Health and Physical Education, Family and Consumer Sciences, Guidance, Fine Arts, Technology, and

World Languages should have performance standards and assessments that apply the same policies and principles as courses in Language Arts, Mathematics, Science, and Social Studies.

The purposes for measurement instruments and exercises include summative, formative, and diagnostic evaluations (Bloom, Hastings, and Madaus, 1971). Instruments and exercises are structured and organized to measure both initial learning shortly after instruction (immediately or a few weeks) and retention of learning some time after instruction (several months or more). Instruments and exercises include test items that require students to *select* a response (for example, multiple-choice items) as well as those that require students to *supply* the response (for example, fill-in-the-blank, an essay, or a project). Measurement exercises that require students to create their own responses may have a wide range in the size of the response expected. In some instances, the time may be very short, a few minutes to create a short paragraph or short essay. In other assessment situations, the time may be much longer, an hour or more or several weeks or months for longer essays, term papers, or projects. There is variation in the number of learner outcomes that are measured. Multiple-choice test items focus on a single learner outcome. When the student creates the response, the number of learner outcomes measured by the exercise varies with the size and time allowed for the exercise.

The course assessment program includes both external and internal measures; that is, those created outside the school or district, such as state tests or commercially available norm-reference or criterion-referenced tests, and those created within the school and district by teachers, such as end-of-unit tests, projects, final exams, quizzes, and homework. Both external and internal instruments should be included in the course assessment program. External measures add credibility to the findings of internal measures. Norm-referenced measures are also a useful part of the assessment program. Comparison to the achievement of other individuals or groups is good information to have when making judgments about students and about the quality of the curriculum and instruction. In some subject areas and courses, external measures may be difficult or even impossible to find. However, they should be used, when they are available.

96

The purpose of the focus of the assessment program at the course level is to ensure that teachers working in teams have data for the purpose of *frequently monitoring student achievement*. The team uses the data to make judgments about each student's achievement and progress toward meeting end-of-course performance standards. Ravitch (2006) calls these end-of-course expectations "performance standards" indicating that they are established by setting performance levels, or "cutting scores," on specific measures. In this way she makes a useful distinction between *content standards* established in state and national standards documents and *performance standards,* which are established by cutting scores on tests (or other types of assessments) and indicate what is superior, acceptable, or unacceptable performance. The need is to frequently measure progress toward meeting performance standards established by policies such the No Child Left Behind (NCLB) legislation. While NCLB has focused initially on reading and math in grades 4 through 8, with intended expansion into other academic areas and to the high school, we advocate that local school districts should establish performance standards for all subject areas at all grade levels; that is, for all courses. The teaching teams use the data from course level assessment programs to make judgments about each student's progress toward meeting performance standards and about the quality of instruction. Teams also use the data to make decisions about the next instructional steps for students who are having difficulty.

Again, each course has its own assessment program. The aggregate of course assessment programs in a school is the *school* assessment program. The aggregate of school assessment programs is the *district* assessment program.

Application of *Assessment Program*

Figure 3-1 presents an assessment framework by listing measurement instruments and exercises that may be found in an assessment program for a course. In an ideal world, most or all of the list would be used in a course. As a practical matter, some types of test are not available for some courses, and it takes time to develop a full range of measurement instruments and exercises.

Figure 3-1. Framework for a Course Level Assessment Program

Instrument	Purpose	Administration Schedule	Comment
External Measures			
State Tests (Criterion-Referenced)	• Measure performance against criteria (standard) • Measure retention of learning	Spring – Last month of school	State test are external but are not likely to be available for all subject areas or courses. Tests may cover more than one course in a subject area. Efforts should be made to disaggregate items to look at course results.
Norm-Referenced Tests	Rank individual students and groups by achievement and compare to the national or state norm groups	Near the end of a school year	These external tests are not likely to be available for all subject areas or courses. Tests may cover more than one course in a subject area. Efforts should be made to disaggregate items to look at course results.
Internal Measures – Tracking Progress Toward Performance Standards			
District Tests (Criterion-Referenced)	• Measure performance against criteria (performance standard) • Measure retention of learning • Measures individual student growth when used as pre- and post-test	Pretest: Fall – First two weeks of school Post-test: Spring – Last two weeks of school	District tests may not be available for all subject areas or courses. When available, tests serve as pre-tests and could serve as all or part of an end-of-course test (or final exam). Pre-test data may be used for students' Personal Plans for Progress.
End-of-Course Tests (Criterion-Referenced)	• Measure performance against standard • Measure retention of learning	End of the course	End-of-course test serves as a final exam and could consist of select and supply type items.
Projects (Criterion-Referenced)	• In-depth measure of several learner outcomes • Measure higher-order thinking	Assessment completion during or at the end of a major unit of instruction, end of quarter, or end of course	• Projects have specific quality criteria and rubrics to guide judgments of quality. • Projects are useful in assessing the integration of more than one subject area into an instructional unit
End-of-Quarter Tests (Criterion-Referenced)	• Measure student mastery of learner outcomes • Monitor student growth • Measure retention of learning	End of the quarter	End-of-quarter test serves as a mid-term exam and could consist of select and supply type items.
End of Unit Tests (Criterion-Referenced)	• Measure student mastery of learner outcomes of the unit • Monitor student growth	End of the unit of instruction	End-of-unit test could consist of select and supply type items.
Formative Assessments Homework Quizzes (Criterion-Referenced)	• Measure student progress toward mastery of learner outcomes • Instructional decision-making for individual students	During instructional units	Formative assessments are used to frequently monitor student progress and quickly respond when students have difficulties or are off target.

As with the curriculum framework, there is more than one useful assessment program framework. When an assessment framework is selected, it should, however, meet these two criteria:

1. Data from assessments must be *frequently* available to teaching teams so that when students are having difficulty, adjustments to instruction can be made quickly.
2. The assessments must give information regarding each student's progress toward the performance standards for the course so that teachers know whether or not students are "on track" for success.

The assessment program also defines the technical writing rules that are used to write test items and exercises. It is beyond the scope of this book to deal with the technical writing rules for the various types of items and exercises. It is, however, important that such rules are established and used consistently for assessments across all subject areas and grade levels.

Assessment Development

Definition and Principles

Assessment development is the process of creating internal and selecting external measurement instruments and exercises for the assessment program. Selection and creation of measurement instruments and exercises are done so that there is alignment (content validity) with the learner outcomes of the curriculum for which performance is to be measured. Assessment development is the process used to select or write the measurement items and exercises used to determine whether and to what extent the learning results established by *essential learnings* and *high expectations* in *all* subject areas for *all* students have been met.

When teachers write test items and exercises for internal assessments, they follow the technical rules for writing that are established in the Assessment Framework. Depending on the purpose and nature of the behavior described in the learner outcomes being measured, test items may be (1) multiple choice, (2) short answer, (3) a product evaluated against established criteria, (4) a performance observed by a judge and evaluated against established criteria, or (5) a survey completed by a group of students anonymously. In some cases, more than one type of item or exercise will be appropriate.

Assessment development applies the principle of embedding assessment in instruction whenever possible. Assessment as a normal part of the instructional process, particularly formative assessment, immediately provides teachers with critical information about student learning and allows teachers to quickly adjust instruction for individuals or groups.

Application of *Assessment Development*

Historically, assessment development has not been well organized in schools. Assessment development at the district level has usually focused on selecting commercial tests, using state mandated tests, and, perhaps, developing district tests. Systematic assessment development at the school level is rare, and development has usually been left to individual teachers working in isolation. As with curriculum development, the knowledge and skill of teachers and leaders at the district and school levels for assessment development is frequently, but not always, low. Assessment development has not been a high priority in teacher or administrator preparation. The result is that teachers, who need to do much of the work of assessment development, and principals, who need to have knowledge and involvement in assessment development, are often not well prepared for this important task. How can the shortage of knowledge and resources for assessment development be overcome? A *redesign* of the organization and structure is needed.

In a school that has been redesigned to provide teams of teachers with one third of the school day as preparation time, some of that time is focused on assessment development and professional growth of the team toward more effective assessment practices. Professional development of *all* teachers and principals is required to ensure understanding of the assessment program framework and capacity of *all* teachers and principals to write measurement items and exercises and to structure them into effective assessment instruments.

When courses are taught in more than one school or by more than one teacher, the subject area teachers collaborate in assessment development so that assessments for a given course are the same whenever and wherever the course is offered. This collaboration within *a subject area department* across schools is important so that there is consistency and fairness of assessment among all students taking a course. This collaborative effort also involves, and coordinates the work of, many teachers in the assessment development task.

Alignment With Curriculum

Definition and Principles

Ensuring that measurement instruments and exercises are aligned with the curriculum they are intended to measure is ensuring *content validity*; that is, the test items or exercises actually measure learning with respect to the learner outcomes that they are intended to measure. This is critical for effective use of the assessment data in making accurate judgments about students' learning, decisions about the quality of instruction, and determining how to improve instruction.

Content validity in this context is based on qualitative judgments made by knowledgeable people; it is a jury process. The "jurors" review the learner outcomes with which the assessment items or exercises are "allegedly" aligned and make judgments about the quality of the alignment. In the context of development of internal measures, the "jurors" are teachers of the subject area, but not the author of the item or exercise. Critical to content validity and alignment of assessment with curriculum is alignment of the taxonomy categories of learner outcomes and measurement items and exercises. There are options regarding taxonomy categories. The cognitive taxonomy developed by Bloom (1956), the affective taxonomy developed by Krathwohl et al. (1964), and the psychomotor taxonomy developed by Simpson (1972) are widely used.

101

Application of *Alignment with Curriculum*

The skills and concepts taken from the content standards documents and the learner outcomes of the curriculum form the basis for judging the alignment of external assessment instruments that might be selected. External tests will usually not measure all the learner outcomes for a course. They will measure a sample of learner outcomes. In the case of state developed tests, one would expect the alignment to be accurate, but the fact is that teachers do not always feel that these tests measure the most important outcomes. In the case of commercial tests, total alignment may be unrealistic. It is likely that there are items on these tests that measure learner outcomes that were not taught. In any case, a careful review of the alignment will provide information about what is measured, what is not, and what is measured that may not have been taught. Everybody involved in using the data from these tests should know that compromises may have been made in alignment which have consequences for interpretation and use of the data.

For internally developed assessment measures, teachers use the learner outcomes to write test items and exercises. Through a peer review process, judgments are made regarding the quality of alignment between assessment items and exercises and the learner outcomes they are intended to measure. When alignment is judged to need improvement, those items and exercises are revised and reviewed again.

Teachers are the primary workers in aligning assessment with curriculum. When possible, it is helpful to involve outside curriculum experts in the various subject areas and assessment experts in making the alignment judgments. This can add a measure of outside credibility to internal assessment development.

Accountability

Definition and Principles

The dictionary describes accountability as the *obligation* to accept responsibility for actions and results. This obligation in schools applies to teachers, administrators, students, parents, and community members. They are accountable for students' achievement of a rigorous curriculum, for graduation, and for success in future education and careers (Fine and Somerville; as cited in Cotton, 2004).

Reeves (2002) points out: "Although it is true that the vast majority of state educational accountability systems refer exclusively to test scores, attendance, school safety, and dropout rate, there is not a single school in the nation that is prohibited from placing those numbers in context by systematically evaluating additional variables in teaching, leadership, and curriculum" (p. 155). Accountability goes beyond measurement of *ends*; accountability does not just apply to learning results. Teaching teams and teachers are accountable for their instructional decisions, teaching pedagogy selected, and the quality of implementation of teaching pedagogy. Accountability must include measures of *means* as well as *ends*. By doing so, insight into relationships between ends and means, which may or may not be cause and effect, is obtained. This leads to more effective decisions about how to improve the instructional *means* in order to improve the achievement of curricular *ends*. Therefore, data must be collected on means variables as well. Reeves (2002) puts it this way:

- Good results with no understanding of reasons are just *luck* and there is little probability of replicating the good results.
- Poor results with no understanding of reasons are *losing* situations.
- Poor results with clear understanding of reasons provide opportunities for *learning* and reduce the probability that mistakes will be duplicated.
- Good results with clear understanding of reasons are examples of *leading* and replications are highly probable.

Application of *Accountability*

In the school/education context, who is accountable for what? The primary players are leaders, teachers, students, and parents. Each member of these groups has a role to play and actions to take for which each member has an obligation to take responsibility and to accept accountability. In the context of this book, we focus on responsibilities related to instruction, curriculum, and assessment.

Leaders in schools and districts have an obligation to take responsibility for the learning results described in the curriculum. For example, the superintendent is accountable for the learning results of *all* students enrolled in the district for the entire K-12 curriculum; a middle school principal is accountable for the learning results of *all* students enrolled in the middle school for the entire curriculum of the grade levels assigned to the school. Superintendents and principals accept this responsibility for learning results by frequently monitoring student progress toward performance standards and taking appropriate leadership action when learning results are *on track* or when learning results are *off track*.

Leaders are also responsible for their leadership activities and decisions. These are discussed in Chapter 5. Generally, these *leadership activities and decisions* relate to the processes of planning, development, implementation, and evaluation focused on improving curriculum, assessment, instruction, and professional practice of themselves as leaders and teachers.

A critically important feature of the redesigned school is an organization that features interdisciplinary teaching teams with collective, shared accountability for the learning results of *all* the students with respect to the entire curriculum assigned to the team. The acceptance of shared responsibility and accountability by each member of the team is critical to the team's ultimate effectiveness; that is, actually achieving the learning results (Katzenbach and Smith, 1993; Covey, 2004). The teaching team and individual teachers are accountable for *implementing decisions and activities* related to the processes of planning, development, implementation, and evaluation focused on improving curriculum, assessment, instruction, and the professional practice of the team and of individual team members.

Students are obligated first to take responsibility and be accountable for their own efforts to learn. As they progress through the grades and increase in maturity, they take on increasing levels of accountability for decision-making for instruction, for curriculum (courses) selected, and for learning results. By doing so, they become increasingly independent learners who are able to judge the quality of their learning accurately and determine what steps are needed next to reach their learning goals.

Parents are the first teachers of children. Through their efforts most children achieve remarkable learning results by the time they enter elementary schools: language development for speaking and listening, social development, and psychomotor development. When children reach school age, parents *delegate* a significant part of the instructional responsibility to schools, but parents should not *abdicate* their responsibility for the continued learning growth of their children. As a practical matter in the first decade of the 21st century, parent responsibility and involvement in the education of their children is not usually high, particularly for students who are having the most difficulty in school. Therefore, schools and teachers must take responsibility for bringing parents and families back into the education of their children by fostering "deeper, more robust connections with families and communities" (Copeland and Boatright, 2004, p. 768).

Accountability is dependent upon data. The assessment program is intended to provide data for learning results. Curriculum documents, instructional plan documents, observations of instruction by leaders and teachers, and teachers' reflective conversations about instruction provide rich, although frequently qualitative, sources of data regarding instructional practices used and the quality of the implementation of those practices. Without data for both results and processes, informed judgments about the quality of results and processes as well as decision-making about improvement are hampered. Lack of time has been the enemy of accountability and improvement processes. By redesigning schools to organize teachers into teams and by providing increased common preparation time for teams, the important tasks of accountability can be greatly strengthened.

Frequently Monitoring Student Achievement

Definition and Principles

Monitoring student achievement takes place at the student, teacher, teaching team, school, and district levels. Parents also play an important role in monitoring the learning progress of their children. The *frequency* of monitoring is greatest at the student, teacher, and team levels, daily or several times a week; but principals and superintendents monitor student achievement at least weekly and monthly, respectively. Edmonds (1979) was among the early researchers to notice and report the positive relationship between frequent monitoring of achievement and the learning results achieved in schools. The call for monitoring student achievement continues from researchers and experts today (Reeves, 2005b; Marzano et al., 2005).

Just *looking at* the data, however, is not all there is to frequently monitoring student achievement. A study called *Why Some Latino Children BEAT THE ODDS...and Other Don't* (Waits, Campbell, Gau, Jacobs, Rex, and Hess, 2006), which replicated the methodology that Jim Collins (2001) used in his study of companies that went from "good to great" with respect to results achieved, describe what happens with data in successful schools:

> The key, however, is not simply that the successful schools have data—it's who is using the data and how they use that data. The schools are deeply engaged in their own assessments in a way that can only be characterized as embedded. There is much, much more to the data analysis than simply looking at the aggregate test scores and exit exams at the end of the year, when it's too late to solve problems. Principals and teacher are collecting and poring over many metrics and

106

measurements. They are doing it over and over, often every week or every month, to make sure they are catching problems as they arise (p. 28).

Application of *Frequently Monitoring Student Achievement*

In the redesigned school, the assessment program of each course provides the data for frequently monitoring student achievement. Teachers in interdisciplinary teaching teams review the results of students' work, including homework, quizzes, projects, and tests administered at the end of an instructional unit, quarterly, or at the end of a course. This variety and frequency of obtaining data about students' progress toward performance standards allows teachers to identify learning difficulties of individual students and to respond quickly with new instruction that is enlightened by the perspectives of several teachers who know the student well. By passing data along to principals and superintendents, leaders become aware of progress toward performance standards and are able to more effectively play their leadership roles for meeting expectations for learning results.

When schools are redesigned to allow time for teachers to do this critically important *evaluation* and *improvement* work in a collaborative environment, there is opportunity to *plan, develop,* and *implement* increasingly effective instruction. The *evaluation* and *improvement* processes use disaggregated data from learning results so that teachers "can look individually at each classroom, each teacher, and most importantly, at each student" (Waits et al., 2006, p. 28) as well as data for the quality of implementation of the instructional processes and resources that were used. The likely result is quickly solving current instructional problems and improved instruction in the future leading to higher levels of student achievement.

Reporting Assessment Results

Definition and Principles

Assessment results are defined by the performance objectives for the student, teacher, teaching team, school, and district. At the student level, the objectives for an individual student to meet are the performance standards set for the courses in which he or she is enrolled. In some Academic Subject Areas, these performance standards are set by "cut scores" on state tests. For other subject areas, the performance standards are set locally during the curriculum and assessment development processes. *All* courses should have performance standards. In cases where state tests are not available to set or measure the performance standards, the performance standards are the "cut scores" on one or more tests or project assessment exercises for the course. There can be more than one cut score indicating gradations of performance such as superior, acceptable, and unacceptable. "Raising the bar" for individual student achievement is done by increasing cut scores or the difficulty level of the measures.

For a course, the performance level to be achieved becomes the *percent of students* who score at or above the cut score, however that was defined for the course. In order to "raise the bar" for the teachers, schools, and districts, the percent of students who must meet or exceed the performance standard is increased. "Closing the gap" among various "groups of interest" requires raising the percent of students who meet or exceed the performance standard in the lower performing groups. Among the groups of interest are those formed by students' racial, ethnic, gender, and socio-economic characteristics.

It is also important to be able to report *growth in achievement* when students begin far below the minimum acceptable performance standard, make significant progress toward the performance standard, but still fall short of the acceptable level. This is important contextual data for interpreting the percent of students meeting the performance standard (Reeves, 2005a).

Assessment results must be reported in a manner that is timely and useful. The audiences for assessment data include, students, teachers, parents, principals, superintendents, school board members, community, and state and federal officials. The first and most important reporting of assessment data is to students, teachers, and parents. They need the most frequent reporting and are the most important users of assessment data. Students, teachers, and parents are the audiences that do the work of teaching and learning and that are in the best position to make good decisions about next steps in the instruction of students, both those who may be having difficulty learning and those who are not. Parents need frequent reports on the progress of their children so that they may support the school's instructional efforts.

School principals need assessment data frequently, too. In their role as supervisor of the implementation of curriculum, assessment, and instruction in the school, they must have first-hand knowledge of how well students are progressing toward meeting the performance standards and what actions are being taken by teachers and teams to deal with problems and issues.

Superintendents also need to know how well students in the district are progressing toward meeting the performance standards set for achievement in each subject area at each grade level. This information is critical to the superintendent's role of supervising principals. In addition, the information is necessary for keeping the board of education and the general public informed about the performance of schools and for accountability to taxpayers. Superintendents also play an important role in communicating learning results to meet state and federal requirements.

Data are originally captured at the student level. As assessment data are reported through the school to the district, local community, and state and federal governments, it must be summarized in meaningful ways to give information about the accomplishment of objectives established for the school and district. These objectives, particularly under NCLB, appropriately relate to *raising the achievement bar* and *closing the achievement gaps* among students over time. But when data are summarized, the ability to "unsummarize" must also exist. The principal and superintendent must be able to ask more specific questions as they work their supervisory roles and "drill down" into the data of their reports to get the answers.

Disaggregation of data is particularly important. First, as noted above, disaggregation of data with respect to student groups of interest is important for determining objective achievement. Second, it is important to disaggregate assessment data relative to learner outcomes. This is important for individual students because it helps to pinpoint specific strengths and weakness in the student's learning of the curriculum. It also helps teachers to determine the strengths and weaknesses of instruction. Third, being able to disaggregate data by learner characteristics such as reading performance, learning style, past performance in the subject area, etc., is helpful in developing new instruction for students having difficulties.

Assessment reporting must also include data about process; i.e., instruction used to achieve student learning results. Sources of these data are observations, documents, and conversations. Observations include watching and recording the activities and interactions of teachers and students. Documents include lesson plans, assessment tools, and teaching materials. Conversations include those observed among teachers on a team and those between teachers and the principal in which the principles and rationale for decisions about teaching are expressed.

Application of *Assessment Reporting*

Reporting assessment data in a timely manner and in a useful format for the intended audience is a critical aspect of the redesigned school. This is particularly true at the student and teacher levels because these are the most important users of the data. Teachers and students make judgments about mastery and progress toward meeting the performance standards of courses, and teachers take corrective action quickly when problems appear.

110

The type of reporting described above as appropriate and helpful may also be problematic in some schools. The information-processing requirement is beyond the "memory capacity" of most teachers and the "paper" record keeping systems they have traditionally used. There are two important sources of help for teachers and others. First, put students, as they are able from growth and maturity perspectives, in charge of their own data and the processing required for disaggregating data with respect to learner outcomes. This has the benefit of students looking at their performance, analyzing it, and learning to make accurate judgments about their progress and performance. Putting students in charge of their own data, however, does not go very far in solving the information-processing problem of reporting meaningful data summaries to principals, superintendents, and the community. Redesigning the school includes systems and processes for reporting assessment data and information to the full spectrum of audiences. The use of computer-based information systems is helpful in this regard (NASSP, 2004; Cawelti, 1997). These systems (1) capture data at the student and teacher levels relatively easily; (2) store the data in ways that accommodate and maintain important relationships among data elements, (3) manipulate data to create meaningful summaries and statistics; and (4) report data summaries and statistics appropriately for the intended audiences. It is beyond the scope of this book to deal with the design and specifications of student, curriculum, and assessment information processing and management systems. There are, however, numerous systems available and in use in many schools.

Responsibility for Assessment Development

Assessments have important connections to both curriculum and instruction. Assessments measure the quality of learning relative to the curriculum. Therefore, they help to define the *ends* or results toward which the school is working. In this context, assessment is connected to curriculum policy and is a district responsibility because school boards set policy. With respect to instruction, assessments can have great value in helping to clarify expectations and in diagnosing strengths and weaknesses during instruction. This is the concept of "embedded assessment," where assessment is a part of the *means*, the instructional processes, and is a teacher responsibility.

Through policy, the board of education should address the assessment practices described in this chapter:

1. Describe the *assessment program and framework*, its characteristics and principles.
2. Establish *assessment development* principles, including *alignment with curriculum*, for selection of external assessments and writing internal assessments.
3. Establish the practice of *frequently monitoring student achievement*.
4. Establish principles of *accountability* and *reporting of test results*.

As with a major portion of curriculum development, the district must take responsibility for coordinating and facilitating selection of external assessment instruments, writing of internal assessments, and final acceptance of them. Teachers, however, will be the primary workers in selecting and writing assessments that follow the policies established by the board of education. The district leaders and school principals have important roles in judging how well these assessments conform to board policy.

Chapter 4: Summary and Concluding Remarks

In this chapter we have described important assessment practices. These practices become the basis for a school district's policies with respect to assessment. Principals and teachers, however, are participants in the development of these policies, and teachers are the primary workers for selecting and writing instruments and exercises.

The practice of *frequently monitoring student achievement* cannot be stressed enough. It has been over 25 years since this critical aspect of high performing schools was identified by Ron Edmonds (Edmonds, 1979).

There must be some means by which pupil progress can be frequently monitored . . .some means must exist in the school by which the principal and the teachers

112

remain constantly aware of pupil progress in relationship to instructional objectives. (p. 22)

Marzano et al. (2004) found that *monitoring* by the principal of school practices (means) with respect to their impact on student learning (ends) is positively and significantly correlated with student achievement. Reeves (2005a) identifies *monitoring* as an essential decision area of effective leaders. And most recently, the *Beat the Odds* study (Waits et al., 2006) found that in successful schools "teachers and principals alike assess student and teacher achievement early and often—and use the information to drive improvement rather than to assign blame" (p. 28).

This latter study placed great emphasis on the rigorous effort that must be applied by principals and teachers to analyze the data, disaggregate the data, reflect upon their meaning and implications, and act to overcome the problems identified (Waits et al., 2006). None of these studies discuss *how* this critical aspect of successful schools happens; that is, where the time comes from or how teachers and principals get together to do this important task. Redesigning the school with at least one third of the school day for teaching teams to work, in part, on *evaluating* and *improving instruction* creates opportunity for this practice to become a regular, routine part of the way education business is conducted in the school – to become part of the school's culture. Without the increased common team time, the likelihood of frequent monitoring of student progress and solving the instructional problems that arise is very low.

Questions for Consideration

1.   What percent of all courses taught in your school have performance standards?
2.   What are your professional growth needs relative to assessment?
3.   How frequently do you monitor student achievement?
4.   How well is student achievement data used to support instructional improvement and report to the community?

5.   To what extent do leaders, teachers, students, and parents feel an obligation to take, and actually do take, responsibility for learning results?

Chapter 5 – Leading the Redesign of a School

> We have to shock the system. We have a duty to expose the system where it is clearly ineffectual…As things are now, we don't even pretend to improve most of our schools; we only talk about it.
>
> (Schmoker; as cited in Reeves, 2006, p. 4)

> Level 5 leaders embody a paradoxical mix of personal humility and professional will. They are ambitious, to be sure, but ambitious first and foremost for the company, not themselves.
>
> (Collins, 2001, p. 39)

In the previous four chapters, we have described practices for each of the three key design elements of schools starting with instruction and followed by curriculum and assessment. We began with the design element of instruction because changing the organization of teachers and students and the structure of time in the school day is essential to creating and sustaining small learning communities and teacher collaboration. Restructuring the organization of teachers, students, and time, allows and facilitates the implementation of a significant amount (one third of the student school day) of *common preparation time* for interdisciplinary teaching teams. It is during this collaborative time that teaching teams focus their collective attention and wisdom on planning, developing, implementing, and evaluating for the purpose of improving curriculum, assessment, instruction, and professional practice. The practices described in Chapters 1 through 4 are among the important practices that principals and teachers need to implement through collaborative approaches to their learning new skills. Research shows that these practices relate to increased student achievement, and they are advocated by prominent educational organizations and experts. Although the practices have been advocated for many years (decades in some cases) they are not being implemented in most schools. We have argued that the current organizational design of teachers, students, and time in most schools does not allow for sustainable implementation of small learning communities and teacher collaboration. The current design supports teacher isolation and inhibits effective teamwork focused on curriculum, assessment, and instruction, and therefore, must be changed – that is, *redesigned*.

In this chapter, we focus on leadership and implementation processes that facilitate the redesign of schools. First we introduce some "acquirable" leader characteristics and actions that facilitate change and support increased student achievement. This is followed by an illustration of a relatively simple strategic planning tool and process that creates *aligned* plans throughout the school district. It the potential to involve *all* district leaders, principals, team leaders and teachers, and even students. The involvement of each individual is focused on that individual's responsibilities for achieving learning results.

Leadership

It is well established that leadership can make a significant difference in student achievement in schools. (Cotton, 2003; Leithwood, Louis, Anderson, and Wahlstrom, 2004; Marzano, et al., 2005) Leithwood et al. identify "basics of successful leadership" from various sources. They describe three: setting direction, developing people, and redesigning the organization.

Applied to schools, *setting direction* involves developing a shared understanding of the school's organization, activities, and the goals that are the purpose of the school – teaching and learning. The importance of direction setting by leaders is that people are motivated by goals that are personally compelling, challenging, and achievable (Leithwood et al., 2004).

It is critical that leaders *develop people*. In schools, teachers must either develop, or already possess, the capacity to apply instructional, curricular, and assessment practices that have high potential for helping a diverse student population learn successfully. The leader's ability to help develop people depends, in part, on the leader's knowledge of the technical core of schooling; that is, *knowledge* of curriculum, instruction, and assessment. Marzano et al. (2005) adds *involvement in design and implementation* to these basics. Other leadership practices mentioned by Leithwood et al. (2004) that significantly and

116

positively help develop people are intellectual stimulation, individualized support, and modeling.

Leaders must create an organization that effectively supports and sustains the performance of leaders (administrators), teachers, and students. The *redesigning the organization* category is derived from recent evidence of the positive effects on student learning of the concepts of "learning organization" and "professional learning community." Organizational cultures and structures must be aligned with the instructional, curricular, and assessment practices that are on the school's improvement agenda. Related leadership practices include strengthening cultures, modifying organizational structures, and building collaborative processes (Leithwood et al. 2004).

Reeves (2005a) discusses leadership in the context of leader decision-making that is subject to developmental modification; that is, leadership skills that can be learned and improved over time. There are four essential leadership decision categories: inquiry, focus, monitoring, and recognition. Leaders decide what they will inquire about (talk about); what their focus will be; what they will measure and monitor; and what they will recognize positively or negatively.

Inquiry deals with understanding the processes and inputs that achieve learning results and those that do not. Leaders need to *decide* to speak with teachers formally and informally about

- instructional practices that will work best with specific subject areas and student learning problems,
- what adults in the school can do to improve learning results, and
- evidence describing student learning results.

Marzano et al. (2005) identify several leadership responsibilities that correlate with student academic achievement that are similar to inquiry:

- Intellectual Stimulation – Leaders ensure faculty and staff are aware of the most current theories and practices and make the discussion of these a regular aspect of the school's culture.

- Ideals/Beliefs – Leaders communicate and operate from strong ideals and beliefs about schooling.

- Optimizer – Leaders inspire and lead new and challenging innovations.

- Change Agent – Leaders are willing to challenge and actively challenge the status quo.

- Involvement in Curriculum, Instruction, and Assessment – Leaders are directly involved in the design and implementation of curriculum, instruction, and assessment practices.

Focus should be on learning results and how to increase the level of performance of all students. For example, increasing the percent of students meeting performance standards is an important objective and focus for a school. The curriculum of the school and the performance standards establish the learning expectations and the required performance level. Also included in *focus* is the alignment of organizational activities, such as professional development; and resources, such as budget and staff; with the learning results described in the curriculum. Marzano et al. (2005) identified *focus* as an important leader responsibility, where the leader "establishes clear goals and keeps those goals in the forefront of the school's attention" (p. 42). It is critical that these goals be specific and measurable.

Monitoring refers to checking progress of students with respect to learning results and monitoring the implementation of instructional processes and inputs. Monitoring learning results will keep the focus on the purpose of the school – student learning. Monitoring processes and inputs informs both what instructional practices and resources were used and the effectiveness of their implementation. It is important to catch instructional errors as early as possible and have information to guide problem solving.

An important quality of monitoring is *frequency*. Frequently monitoring student achievement has long been associated with school effectiveness (Edmonds, 1979). At the teacher and student levels, monitoring frequency must be at least weekly as well as monthly, quarterly, semi-annually, and yearly. Reeves (2005a) makes the point that there is perhaps too much end-of-year testing and that more classroom testing during the school year is needed so that data are available for frequent monitoring of student progress and adjusting instruction when necessary. Following student progress is a practice that applies throughout the educational organization from the superintendent to principal to teacher to student. Frequent monitoring of student achievement at each of these levels is critical for accountability and improvement of results.

Recognition can be both positive and negative, but the balance should be tipped toward positive (Reeves, 2005a). Marzano et al. (2005) identified two responsibilities related to *recognition* that are positively correlated with student achievement:

- Affirmation – Leaders recognize and celebrate accomplishments and acknowledge failures.
- Contingent Rewards – Leaders recognize and reward individual accomplishments.

We have only touched on leadership briefly, but the practices, decisions, and responsibilities identified are well researched and prominent in the literature because of their relationship to improved student achievement. When leaders (1) set direction that focuses on learning results; (2) develop people's knowledge and skills in effective instructional, curricular, and assessment practices; (3) redesign the organization to support small learning communities and teacher collaboration; and (4) make appropriate decisions about inquiry, focus, monitoring, and recognition; there is high probability that learning results will improve. All of these are important leadership issues, but there is at least one more.

Leaders must be bold and they must be willing to lead significant change that has enough magnitude to make a meaningful difference. Efforts to create small learning communities that are shallow, which do too little too slowly, or where changes are incremental supplements or add-ons to existing arrangements, usually fail. Experienced practitioners and researchers recommend implementing as many of the practices as possible as quickly as possible. What is needed is a clean, bold break with the past, not timid incrementalism (Cotton, 2004). Cawelti (1997) put it this way: "My own analysis of the research literature on high school restructuring concludes that certain *individual* changes produce higher student achievement (albeit modest in size based on single changes), but that we can expect much larger increments of improvement when a school is able to simultaneously accomplish changes in most or all of the critical elements described here" (page 15). (See Appendix A for a list of Cawelti's critical elements.) The first *Breaking Ranks* (NASSP, 1996) voiced the same concern, which was repeated in *Breaking Ranks II*™ (NASSP, 2004):

> The cause of reform is hobbled by the inclination of educational institutions to resist substantial change…What passes as change is frequently no more than tinkering around the edges…It is not by accident that this report titles itself *Breaking Ranks* (p. xvii).

Tinkering around the edges of school reform is ill advised. In order for change to be sustainable, it must create a culture of change and take note of the interdependence of new practices; that is, implementing one best practice may *require* the implementation of others.

The One Page® Strategic Planning Model

We now turn to implementation of the *instructional, curricular*, and *assessment* practices that have been advocated and described in this book. These practices have sound backing for their potential to increase student achievement. Applying the leadership practices described in the first part of this chapter will play an important role in their effective implementation.

120

A *plan*, however, is necessary to set direction for the short and long term. Districts and schools have used various strategic and tactical planning processes, some more formal, some less; some more complex, some less; some more time consuming, some less. We have opted for less complex and less time consuming – that is, a strategic planning process that creates relatively short, simply structured documents that can be written in a relatively short space of time, a few hours over a few days.

We think that "less time consuming" is very important. The need for schools to get better results sooner rather than later is critical. It is critical for our nation, and even more critical for the students who are in our schools now. The planning format and process described here is relatively simple, focused on the learning results, and can be completed in a short period of time.

Also, as just noted in the discussion of leadership, being bold and making multiple, significant changes quickly provides a greater possibility of both success in the short term and sustainability in the long term. We recognize that change often involves a "learning curve" which must be honored; change often requires new understandings and competencies. The speed of change must consider the context, but leaders must be relentless in their pursuit of the objectives and the organizational changes necessary to achieve them.

The strategic planning model and process is taken from Jim Horan's *The One Page Business Plan®* (Horan, 2004). The framework has five equal components: vision, mission, objectives, strategies, and action plans, all of which should fit on *one page*. This framework may be applied at all levels of the educational organization: school district (superintendent), school (principal), teaching team (team leader), individual teacher, and individual student. It is possible for one school or teaching team to be the first to use The One Page® Model, as long as the plans do not conflict with policies and procedures of levels above. Important qualities of this planning process are (1) all plans are aligned, (2) they are focused on student learning, and (3) *everyone* participates in the planning process by writing a plan that is one page long and deals with his or her specific responsibilities.

The One Page® Plan Methodology and Contents

The planning process starts at the *top* of the organization. Ideally, that is the superintendent initiating planning for the district, but it could be a principal planning for a school or a team leader planning for a team. By starting at the top, leaders have an important opportunity to communicate their strongly held beliefs about schools, education, and learning. In doing so, they demonstrate that they *have* strong beliefs and ideals about education. This is an important characteristic of strong educational leaders. It is associated positively and significantly with increased student achievement (Marzano et al. 2005)

The rational for starting at the *top* is to assure alignment of plans across the organizational levels of the school district (or school, or team). Starting at the *top* does not mean that participation of others is unimportant or omitted. First, each leader; superintendent, principal, or team leader; will write a plan for her or his level in the organization. Each individual teacher and student will also write a plan. In this way, participation is guaranteed. Second, the leaders should not write their plans without communicating with the people they lead and gathering data about the present performance of the district, school, or team. This gathering of data, thoughts, and ideas from others can be formal or informal, and the leader gives careful consideration to them when writing the plan. The plan is, however, the leader's plan for the organization or the part of the organization he or she leads. The leader's plan is not written by a committee; it is written by the leader.

After a leader writes her or his plan, it is still considered a draft, albeit a very "polished" draft. That draft is then presented to the people who are led directly by that leader. In the case of the superintendent, this would be district level administrators and school principals. In the case of principals, this would be assistant principals and team leaders in the school. In the case of teaching team leaders, this would be teachers and others on the team. After presentation and discussion, the leader finalizes his or her plan, and the planning process moves to the next level down in the organization. The lapsed time for writing a plan at any level should be about two weeks. Therefore, the plans for an entire district from superintendent to district administrators and school principals to team leaders to teachers will take about two months. Because plans are aligned, they will have aligned *vision and mission* statements that are *clear and shared*.

The writing of One Page Plans by students is part of the instructional practice of Personal Plans for Progress. The knowledge and skills for writing One Page Plans by students is a part of the Guidance curriculum and is taught to students, beginning in elementary schools, during the time allocated to the Personal Decision-Making Teaching Team. Personal Adult Advocates and the families of students play roles in providing input to the plan content, and later, in monitoring progress of the plan.

We introduce the five components of The One Page® framework with references from Jim Horan's descriptions of the components. These descriptions use business terminology, so we follow them with descriptions of the applications in educational organizations. Examples of One Page Plans for the Columbia School District are given in Appendix D.

Vision – What are we building?

> "Vision statements should be expansive and idealistic. They should stimulate thinking, communicate passion, and paint a very graphic picture of the business you want" (Horan, 2004, p. 29). The vision statement addresses questions of what, where, who, when, why, and how.

In an educational organization, we are building an instructional organization (what) that will have a high probability of all students (who) successfully learning the curriculum that is required and chosen by them (why). The instructional organization is built in communities (where) by effectively bringing together human and material resources to deliver instruction focused on the learning described in the curriculum and measured by the instrumentation of the assessment program (how). The educational organization needs to be redesigned *now* (when).

The vision statement should be *bold*. It should stretch your imagination as you work on other components of the plan. It should stimulate others to see new possibilities. When writing vision statements, don't hold anything back. The vision statement should focus on successful student learning.

Mission – Why do we exist?

> "The mission statement describes the purpose for which your product, service, or business exists. Great mission statements are short and memorable...Mission statements are also about commitments and promises" (Horan, 2004, page 39).

Schools provide a service, teaching. The purpose of teaching is successful learning for students. This is the commitment that every school should have and the promise it makes to its constituents. (See the discussion of the concept of "clearly stated vision and mission focused on student learning" in Chapter 3.)

Objectives – What results will we measure?

> "Objectives clarify what it is you are trying to accomplish in specific, measurable goals. For an objective to be effective, it needs to be a well-defined target with quantifiable elements that are measurable...Your objectives are designed to focus your resources on achieving specific results. The purpose of a well-defined objective is to cause meaningful action...Create objectives that can be measured and then measure the results throughout the year. Objectives are a prime tool for accountability" (Horan, 2004, p. 49).

Objectives that focus on learning results are described in detail in the curriculum. They serve to focus resources on the results the district, schools, teaching teams, teachers, and students are trying to achieve. The curriculum provides measurable learner outcomes and the assessment program provides the measures of their achievement. Growth means raising the level of student achievement. It could be raising cutting scores for meeting standards (raising the bar) and/or increasing the proportion of students expected to meet standards (closing the gap). The levels of accomplishment of these objectives have numbers associated with them so that progress can be graphed.

Objectives related to student achievement should state the proportion of students expected to achieve the performance standard. Schools should

1. Increase the proportion of students achieving standards (raising the bar),
2. When benchmark levels are not available, set a target proportion of students expected to achieve standards (setting the bar),
3. Set growth targets for students who do not achieve standards (closing the gap), and
4. Set target proportions of students in subpopulations that will achieve standards (closing the gap).

When thinking about the objectives related to student achievement at different levels in the educational organization, it is important to think about the learning results, described in the curriculum, for which each level is responsible and accountable. In the case of the district level, the superintendent (and his or her team of assistants, associates, directors, etc.) is responsible for the district's *entire* curriculum for *all* of the students in the district. At the school level, the principal (and her or his team of assistants, associates, etc.) is responsible for the school's *entire* curriculum for *all* of the students enrolled in the school. For teaching teams, the team is responsible for the *entire* curriculum assigned to the team for *all* students assigned to the team. Individual teachers are responsible for the curriculum of the subject areas and courses they are assigned to teach and for the learning of students assigned to them. Finally, individual students are responsible for the learning results described in the curriculum of the courses that they are taking at any particular point in their progression through the grade levels.

Objectives should also be set for *parent/community satisfaction* with the school. These objectives should state the percent of parents/community who are satisfied. Schools should

1. Increase the proportion of parents/community who are satisfied with schools (raising the bar),
2. When benchmark levels are not available, set a target proportion of parents/community who are satisfied with schools (*setting* the bar), and
3. Set target proportions for subpopulations of parents/community for satisfaction with schools (closing the gap).

A third important type of objective for educational leaders to set is teacher satisfaction. Objectives should be set to improve the level of teacher satisfaction with their jobs and working conditions.

The objectives are the critical results for which strategies and action plans are written; these are the *results* that will be measured by the assessment program in the case of student learning results and by appropriate survey instruments in the cases of parent/community and teacher satisfaction. The district, schools, teaching teams, teachers, and students will be judged by the data for each objective.

We need to clarify the relationship between teaching team and individual teacher responsibility and accountability. An important characteristic that makes a group of individuals a team is shared responsibility and accountability for *all* the objectives of the team. In the case of small learning communities, the phrase "*all* the objectives" refers to the curriculum of *all* the courses assigned to the team. For example, Academic Team members *all* share responsibility and accountability for students' learning in Language Arts, Mathematics, Science, and Social Studies. The team also has collective/shared accountability for processes used to achieve the curricular goals. Within the team, however, specific teachers will have a subject area specialty (perhaps more than one) for which they take specific responsibility for planning, development, implementation, and evaluation. The distinction here between team and individual responsibility and accountability is the team's collective role in contrast to the individual *diversified roles* played by individual members. Individual team members are responsible for the contributions they need to make as they play one or more of the diversified roles needed by the team. Individual team members are also responsible for the learning results their diversified roles are intended to produce. One role that individual team members play is contributing effectively to the collaborative work of the team, which includes helping to solve instructional problems regardless of the subject area in which they may fall. Through this role team members have accountability for *all* of the team's objectives.

Progress toward achievement of objectives is tracked with scorecards that report the data from the assessment programs. Scorecards are reviewed *frequently*. This is the practice of "frequently monitoring achievement." The frequency of monitoring will vary depending on the level of the organization. At the student and teacher levels, students should be checking their progress, taking into account their maturity and with teacher assistance, almost daily, if not daily. At the teaching team level, monitoring should be at least weekly, with the principal (school level) participating as an observer in the monitoring sessions. The superintendent (district level) monitors school level progress at least monthly.

In addition to objectives for student achievement and parent/community satisfaction, objectives may be set for instructional, curriculum, assessment, and professional development. These objectives relate to critical new processes needed to achieve the desired student learning results. They must be, of course, measurable and "graphable;" that is, they must have numbers that measure progress toward achievement.

Strategies – How will we build this enterprise?

> Strategies are *industry practices*. "Strategies set the direction, philosophy, values, and methodology for building and managing your company...These core strategies are easy to understand, remain relatively constant over time, are used by market leaders, and result in growth" (Horan, 2004, p. 59).

The "company" and its subdivisions in educational organizations are the school district (the company), the schools (subdivisions of the company), teaching teams (operational units within subdivisions), teachers (individual leaders of learning for students within operational units), and individual students (the workers in the K-12 learning organization). Strategies define direction (e.g., implementing best practices for instruction), philosophy (e.g., a collaborative approach), values (e.g., continuous improvement), and methodology (e.g., interdisciplinary teams, training, and coaching). The educational practices that have been described in this book are among the *strategies* that can be used to achieve the learning results identified in the objectives, but they are not necessarily the only ones, as we have stated earlier. They are, however, strategies that have been associated with increasing student achievement. The strategies of The One Page® Plan describe how the objectives will be achieved, and therefore there is alignment between objectives and strategies.

Action Plans – What is the work to be done?

> "Plans are the specific actions the business must implement to achieve the objectives. Plans or action items should be important, significant, and contribute to the growth of your business" (Horan, 2004, p. 71).

Initially, action plans are statements that describe what is to be completed by a project, task, or activity; when it is to be completed; and who is responsible for completion. Each action plan must be directly related to a strategy and an objective. This is "alignment" within each plan. Each action plan will have a progress report with specific tasks, deadlines, and individual responsible.

Managing the implementation of action plans is critical. Failure to implement action plans is a major reason for an organization's failure. Creating progress charts that list the specific steps for completing the action plan is an important exercise. Jim Horan (2004) emphasizes the importance of *frequently monitoring* progress:

> Managing the implementation is…making sure that the actions take place and are in line with the defined strategies, objectives, and plans. Everyone must be held accountable for meeting his or her goals. Frequent reviews and continuous monitoring of results will help move you toward your defined goals. *Failure To Implement* is not acceptable and must be dealt with immediately. (p. 81)

So, the implementation of action plans is monitored *frequently*. Monitoring of action plans is not only for completing actions on time and within budget, but also for the quality of implementation (Did the action taken effectively implement the associated strategy?) and the quality of results (Did the action achieve the intended results?). Actions are taken to implement specific strategies; strategies are selected to achieve specific objectives. Did the strategy work? This is a "cause and effect" question. This monitoring process and cause-

strategy work? This is a "cause and effect" question. This monitoring process and cause-effect analysis is critical to continuous improvement of learning results in the school. When expected progress is not being made, an analysis of the implementation of strategies and action plans is necessary to effectively solve the problem and get back on track.

Chapter 5: Summary and Concluding Remarks

Leaders must lead. Although leaders may not directly impact student learning, it is clear that what they choose to do as leaders does make a difference. The importance of *involvement* of leaders with the school design elements of curriculum, assessment, and instruction is clear from the meta-analysis of research done by Marzano et al. (2005). Leaders must *set direction*, *develop people*, and *redesign the organization* for collaboration (Leithwood et al., 2004). Leaders must make decisions regarding what they will *inquire about*, *focus on*, *monitor*, and *recognize* (Reeves, 2005a). While school leadership may frequently be too large a job for one individual, the top leader of a school, the principal, must continuously demonstrate active involvement in the design and implementation of instruction, curriculum, and assessment.

Redesigning a school requires careful and detailed planning (Cotton, 2004). That planning process needs to create focused objectives and clear action plans for implementing strategies that will lead to achievement of the objectives. Schmoker (2004) has pointed out that many large strategic planning processes have been futile and suggests that *teams* of teachers who make many small improvements on a regular, frequent, and routine basis provide a much better alternative. We agree. This book is about teams of teachers collaborating to improve the learning results of individual students daily and weekly. A plan to *redesign* schools is, however, needed. The One Page® Plan concept, tool, and process provide plans that do not create volumes of paper written by a relatively small committee. Such plans frequently just "sit on the shelf." The One Page® Plan process advocated here involves all participants in writing their own focused plans, which they will implement, monitor, and adjust as needed. The One Page® Model creates brief plans that are focused on learning results, aligned, and involve all players from the superintendent to

plans by monitoring their progress toward, and the accomplishment of, the plans' objectives as well as the quality implementation of the strategies through the action plans.

The questions asked in The One Page® Plan process with regard to vision, mission, objectives, strategies, and action plans are very similar to those asked about mission, vision, values, and goals by DuFour, Dufour, Baker, and Many (2006) in their book *Learning by Doing: A Handbook for Professional Learning Communities at Work.* Figure 5-1 gives a comparison.

Figure 5-1. A Comparison of Plan Components and Questions of DuFour, DuFour, Baker, and Many (2006) and Horan (2004)

DuFour, DuFour, Baker, and Many		Horan	
Plan Components	Questions	Plan Components	Questions
Vision	What must our school become to accomplish our purpose?	Vision	What are we building?
Mission	Why do we exist?	Mission	Why do we exist?
Goals	How will we mark our progress?	Objectives	What results will we measure?
Values	How must we behave to achieve our vision?	Strategies	How will we build this enterprise?
		Action Plans	What is the work to be done?

Examples of The One Page® Plans for the Columbia School District can be found in Appendix D. These examples show focus on learning, alignment among levels, and implementation of practices advocated in this book.

Figure 5-2 gives a summary of the definitions of each component of The One Page® Plan.

Figure 5-2. Components of The One Page® Plan with Descriptions

---

Vision – What are we building?

"Vision statements should be expansive and idealistic. They should stimulate thinking, communicate passion, and paint a very graphic picture of the business you want." (Horan 2004, p. 29) The vision statement addresses questions of what, where, who, when, why, and how.

Mission – Why do we exist?

"The mission statement describes the purpose for which your product, service, or business exists. Great mission statements are short and memorable" (Horan, 2004, p. 39).

Objectives – What results will we measure?

Objectives clarify what it is you are trying to accomplish in specific, measurable goals. For an objective to be effective, it needs to be a well-defined target with quantifiable elements that are measurable….your objectives are designed to focus your resources on achieving specific results. The purpose of a well-defined objective is to cause meaningful action. Create objectives that can be measured and then measure the results throughout the year. Objectives are a prime tool for accountability. (Horan, 2004, p. 49).

Strategies – How will we build this enterprise?

Strategies are *industry practices*. "Strategies set the direction, philosophy, values, and methodology for building and managing your company…These core strategies are easy to understand, remain relatively constant over time, are used by market leaders, and result in growth" (Horan, 2004, p. 59).

Action Plans – What is the work to be done?

"Plans are the specific actions the business must implement to achieve the objectives. Plans or action items should be important, significant, and contribute to the growth of your business" (Horan, 2004, p. 71).

Questions for Consideration

1. What is the nature of inquiry, focus, monitoring, and recognition in your school? How would you like to see it changed, if at all?

2. What leadership behavior in your school supports the concepts of "learning communities" and "collaboration?"

3. To what extent has your school's or district's latest strategic plan been implemented?

4. What evidence is available that your school's or district's latest strategic plan has had an impact on student achievement?

5. What ideas do you have for making the planning process more useful and effective?

6. How would the implementation of he One Page planning methodology help your school or district have a significant impact on student achievement?

Appendix A

Summary Lists of Practices
from the Five Major Sources

Small Learning Communities

New Small Learning Communities: Findings from Recent Literature (Cotton, 2004)

Key Elements for Success of Small Learning Communities

Self-Determination

    Autonomy

    Separateness

    Distinctiveness

    Self-Selection of Teachers and Students

    Flexible Scheduling

Identity

    Vision/Mission

    Focus on Student Learning

    Detailed Planning

Personalization

    Knowing Student Well

    Heterogeneity/Nontracking

    Looping

    Parent and Community Involvement

Support for Teaching

    Leadership/Decision Making

    Professional Development and Collaboration

Integrated Curriculum/Teaching Teams

Large Repertoire of Instructional Strategies

Functional Accountability

Multiple Forms of Assessment

Accountability/Credibility

District, Boards, and Legislatures

Networking with other Small Learning Communities

Thoroughgoing Implementation

Breaking Ranks II™

Breaking Ranks II™: Strategies for Leading High School Reform, (NASSP, 2004)

Seven Cornerstone Strategies to Improve Student Performance

1. Establish the essential learnings a student is required to master in order to graduate, and adjust the curriculum and teaching strategies to realize that goal.

2. Increase the quantity and improve the quality of interactions between students, teachers, and other school personnel by reducing the number of students for which any adult or group of adults is responsible.

3. Implement a comprehensive advisory program that ensures that each student has frequent and meaningful opportunities to plan and assess his or her academic and social progress with a faculty member.

4. Ensure that teachers use a variety of instructional strategies and assessment to accommodate individual learning styles.

5. Implement schedules flexible enough to accommodate teaching strategies consistent with the ways student learn most effectively and that allow for effective teacher teaming and lesson planning.

6. Institute structural leadership changes that allow for meaningful involvement in decision making by students, teachers, family members, and the community and that support effective communication with these groups.

7. Align the schoolwide comprehensive, ongoing professional development program and the individual Personal Learning Plans of staff members with the content knowledge and instructional strategies required to prepare students for graduation.

31 Recommendations

Collaborative Leadership and Professional Learning Communities

1. The principal will provide leadership in the high school community by building and maintaining a vision, direction, and focus for student learning.

2. Each high school will establish a site council and accord other meaningful roles in decision making to students, parents, and members of the staff in order to promote student learning and a atmosphere of participation, responsibility, and ownership.

3. A high school will regard itself as a community in which members of the staff collaborate to develop and implement the school's learning goals.

4. Teachers will provide the leadership essential to the success of reform, collaborating with others in the educational community to redefine the role of the teacher and to identify sources of support for that redefined role.

5. Every school will be a learning community for the entire community. As such, the school will promote the use of Personal Learning Plans for each educator and provide the resources to ensure that the principal, teachers, and other staff members can address their own learning and professional development needs as they relate to improved student learning.

6. The school community will promote policies and practices that recognize diversity in accord with the core values of a democratic and civil society and

will offer substantive ongoing professional development to help educators appreciate issues of diversity and expose students to a rich array of viewpoints, perspectives, and experiences.

7. High schools will build partnerships with institutions of higher education to provide teachers and administrators at both levels with ideas and opportunities to enhance the education, performance, and evaluation of educators.

8. High schools will develop political and financial relationships with individuals, organizations, and businesses to support and supplement educational programs and policies.

9. At least once every five years, each high school will convene a broadly based external panel to offer a public description of the school, a requirement that could be met in conjunction with the evaluations by state, regional, and other accrediting groups.

Personalization and the School Environment

10. High schools will create small units in which anonymity is banished.

11. Each high school teacher involved in the instructional program on a full – time basis will be responsible for contact time with no more than 90 students during a given term so that the teacher can give greater attention to the needs of every student.

12. Each student will have a Personal Plan for Progress that will be reviewed often to ensure that the high school takes individual needs into consideration and to allow students, within reasonable parameters, to design their own methods for learning in an effort to meet high standards

13. Every high school student will have a Personal Adult Advocate to help him or her personalize the educational experience.

14. Teachers will convey a sense of caring so that students feel that their teachers share a stake in student learning.

15. High schools will develop flexible scheduling and student grouping patterns that allow better use of time in order to meet the individual needs of students and to ensure academic success.

16. The high school will engage students' families as partners in the student education.

17. The high school community, which cannot be values-neutral, will advocate and model a set of core values essential in a democratic and civil society.

18. High schools' in conjunction with agencies in the community, will help coordinate the delivery of physical and mental health and social services for youth.

Curriculum, Instruction, and Assessment

19. Each high school will identify a set of essential learnings—in literature and language, writing, mathematics, social studies, science, and the arts—in which students must demonstrate achievement in order to graduate.

20. Each high school will present alternatives to tracking and ability grouping.

21. The high school will reorganize the traditional department structure in order to integrate the school's curriculum to the extent possible and emphasize depth over breadth of coverage.

22. The content of the curriculum, where practical, should connect to real-life applications of knowledge and skills to help students link their education to the future.

23. The high school will promote service programs and student activities as integral to an education, providing opportunities for all students that support and extend academic learning.

24. The academic program will extend beyond the high school campus to take advantage of learning opportunities outside the four wall of the building.

25. Teachers will design high-quality work and teach in ways that engage students, encourage them to persist, and, when the work is successfully completed, result in student satisfaction and their acquisition of knowledge,

critical thinking, and problem solving skills, and other abilities valued by society.

26. Teachers will know and be able to use a variety of strategies and setting that identify and accommodate individual learning styles and engage students.

27. Each high school teacher will have a broad base of academic knowledge with depth in at least one subject area.

28. Teachers will be adept at acting as coaches and facilitators to promote more active involvement of students in their own learning.

29. Teachers will integrate assessment into instruction so that assessment is accomplished using a variety of methods and does not only measure students, but becomes part of the learning process.

30. Recognizing that education is a continuum, high schools will reach out to elementary and middle level schools as well as institutions of higher education to better serve the articulation of student learning and to ensure that at each stage of the continuum, stakeholders understand what will be required of students at the succeeding stage.

31. Schools will develop a strategic plan to make technology integral to curriculum, instruction, and assessment, accommodating different learning styles and helping teachers to individualize and improve the learning process.

Effective Schools Research

Effective Schools Research (Edmonds, 1979 and Taylor, 2002),

The Correlates of Effective Schools

Clearly stated and focused school mission

Safe and orderly climate for learning

High expectations for students, teachers, and administrators

Opportunity to learn and student time-on-task

Instructional leadership by all administrators and staff members

Frequent monitoring of student progress

Positive home/school relations

Critical Elements

Effects of High School Restructuring: Ten Schools at Work (Cawelti, 1997)

Seven Critical Restructuring Elements

Focal Elements of Restructuring

    Curriculum Standards

    Effective Teaching/Active Learning

    Results Orientation: Performance Assessment

Facilitating Elements

    Technology

    Human Resources Development

    Parent-community Involvement

    Work redesign

Balanced Leadership Framework™

Balanced leadership: What 30 years of research tells us about the effect of leadership on student achievement. (Waters, Marzano, and McNulty, 2003)

Balanced Leadership Framework™ Responsibilities

1. Affirmation: Recognizes and celebrates school accomplishments and acknowledges failures

2. Change agent: Is willing to and actively challenges the status quo

3. Communications: Establishes strong lines of communications with teachers and among students

4. Contingent rewards: Recognizes and rewards individual accomplishments

5. Culture: Fosters shared beliefs and a sense of community and cooperation

6. Discipline: Protects teachers from issues and influences that would detract from their teaching time and focus

7. Flexibility: Adapts his or her leadership behavior to the needs of the current situation and is comfortable with dissent

8. Focus: Establishes clear goals and keeps those goals in the forefront of the school's attention

9. Ideals/beliefs: Communicates and operates from strong ideals and beliefs about schooling

10. Input: Involves teachers in the design and implementation of important decisions

11. Intellectual stimulation: Ensures that the faculty and staff are aware of the most current theories and practices and makes the discussion of these a regular aspect of the school culture

12. Involvement in curriculum, instruction, assessment: Is directly involved in the design and implementation of curriculum, instruction, and assessment practices

13. Knowledge of curriculum, instruction, assessment: Is knowledgeable about current curriculum, instruction, and assessment practices

14. Monitor/evaluate: Monitors the effectiveness of school practices and their impact on student learning

15. Optimize: Inspires and leads new and challenging innovations

16. Order: Establishes a set of standard operating procedures and routines

17. Outreach: Is an advocate and spokes person for the school to all stakeholders

18. Relationships: Demonstrates awareness of the personal aspects of teachers and staff

19. Resources: Provides teachers with materials and professional development necessary for the successful execution of their jobs

20. Situational awareness: Is aware of the details and the undercurrents in the running of the school and uses this information to address current and potential problems

21. Visibility: Has quality contacts and interactions with teachers and students

Appendix B

Data for School Districts
Serving State Capital Cities

The data shown in Tables B-1, B-2, B-3, and B-4 were retrieved from the National Center for Education Statistics website: http://nces.ed.gov/ccd/districtsearch/. These data are for school districts that serve state capital cities in the United States. In some cases, capital cities are served by more than one school district. In those cases, we choose one for inclusion. One capital city school district did not have data available.

Table B-1 is an alphabetical listing by state. Table B-2 is the same data as Table B-1 but sorted by student-to-teacher ratio. This table shows the mean student-to-teacher ratio to be 15.2 with a range of 10.3 to 21.3. When counselors and library/media specialists are included with teachers, Table B-3, the median student-to-teacher, counselor, and library/media specialist ratio is 14.4 and the range is 9.6 to 19.8. Table B-4 is sorted by the ratio of teachers-to-instructional aides. This table shows the median teacher-to-instructional aide ratio to be 4.2 with a range of 1.7 to 7.4.

Table B-1. Data for School Districts Serving Capital Cities – Alphabetical Listing by State
Source: National Center for Education Statistics, Common Core of Data, 2003-2004

State	Capital	Students	Teachers	Students Per Teacher	Counselors	Library/Media Specialist	Students Per Teacher, Counselor, &Library/Media Specialist	Instructional Aides	Teachers Per Instructional Aide
Alabama	Montgomery	32,553	2,171.5	15.0	71.0	59.0	14.1	263.5	8.2
Alaska	Juneau	5,475	305.0	18.0	11.5	3.0	17.1	106.5	2.9
Arizona	Phoenix	34,884	1,788.1	19.5	38.0	34.1	18.8	381.4	4.7
Arkansas	Little Rock	25,346	1,726.0	14.7	77.0	49.0	13.7	374.0	4.6
California	Sacramento	52,103	2,659.0	19.6	22.9	13.8	19.3	309.5	8.6
Colorado	Denver	72,100	4,217.8	17.1	69.3	109.0	16.4	1,118.7	3.8
Connecticut	Hartford	22,578	1,717.4	13.1	42.0	37.0	12.6	426.0	4.0
Delaware	Dover	5,909	416.4	14.2	15.0	6.0	13.5	79.1	5.3
Florida	Tallahassee	32,194	1,817.0	17.7	72.0	41.0	16.7	606.0	3.0
Georgia	Atlanta	52,103	3,692.0	14.1	133.0	92.0	13.3	738.0	5.0
Hawaii	Honolulu	183,609	11,128.5	16.5	674.5	290.0	15.2	2,639.7	4.2
Idaho	Boise	26,211	1,466.2	17.9	77.5	11.2	16.9	252.3	5.8
Illinois	Springfield	15,212	944.7	16.1	0.0	7.0	16.0	0.0	
Indiana	Indianapolis	39,989	2,769.8	14.4	67.3	46.9	13.9	532.9	5.2
Iowa	Des Moines	31,086	2,328.5	13.4	88.5	21.0	12.8	534.8	4.4
Kansas	Topeka	14,049	1,071.4	13.1	35.5	31.5	12.3	345.1	3.1
Kentucky	Frankfort	6,026	365.1	16.5	10.0	9.5	15.7	121.3	3.0
Louisiana	Baton Rouge	46,644	3,137.0	14.9	312.0	97.0	13.2	641.0	4.9
Maine	Augusta	2,611	244.7	10.7	10.0	2.0	10.2	99.1	2.5
Maryland	Annapolis	74,508	4,501.1	16.6	196.1	107.8	15.5	625.9	7.2
Massachusetts	Boston	60,150	3,926.3	15.3	229.8	20.5	14.4	787.8	5.0
Michigan	Lansing	16,979							
Minnesota	St. Paul	42,510	2,754.0	15.4	81.4	45.4	14.8	1,195.4	2.3
Mississippi	Jackson	31,640	1,900.8	16.6	88.2	63.2	15.4	532.6	3.6
Missouri	Jefferson City	8,228	570.3	14.4	30.0	16.0	13.4	134.0	4.3
Montana	Helena	8,084	465.0	17.4	11.5	13.8	16.5	50.8	9.2
Nebraska	Lincoln	32,120	2,341.6	13.7	69.9	50.8	13.0	388.4	6.0
Nevada	Carson City	8,798	507.7	17.3	17.0	9.0	16.5	145.4	3.5
New Hampshire	Concord	5,473	339.9	16.1	17.8	5.3	15.1	150.8	2.3
New Jersey	Trenton	13,227	1,017.0	13.0	44.0	18.0	12.3	222.0	4.6
New Mexico	Albuquerque	90,537	6,191.0	14.6	206.2	93.5	13.9	1,532.5	4.0
New York	Albany	9,919	787.4	12.6	14.5	14.6	12.1	269.0	2.9
North Carolina	Raleigh	109,424	7,302.0	15.0	260.0	168.0	14.2	1,727.0	4.2
North Dakota	Bismarck	10,477	662.1	15.8	25.1	12.4	15.0	158.0	4.2
Ohio	Columbus	63,098	3,838.4	16.4	126.8	70.8	15.6	1,096.3	3.5
Oklahoma	Oklahoma City	40,599	2,344.9	17.3	33.3	49.0	16.7	456.3	5.1

Table B-1. Continued.

State	Capital	Students	Teachers	Students Per Teacher	Coun-selors	Library/ Media Specialist	Students Per Teacher, Counselor, &Library/Media Specialist	Instructional Aides	Teachers Per Instructional Aide
Oregon	Salem	37,785	1,772.5	21.3	90.7	49.9	19.8	635.4	2.8
Pennsylvania	Harrisburg	7,883	587.0	13.4	24.0	6.0	12.8	79.0	7.4
Rhode Island	Providence	27,900	1,779.0	15.7					
South Carolina	Columbia	26,990	1,986.8	13.6	87.0	54.0	12.7	448.0	4.4
South Dakota	Pierre	2,670	162.0	16.5	8.0	1.0	15.6	82.4	2.0
Tennessee	Nashville	68,651	4,857.6	14.1	180.5	119.0	13.3	711.0	6.8
Texas	Austin	79,007	5,354.4	14.8	162.1	98.9	14.1	747.0	7.2
Utah	Salt Lake City	24,443	1,229.7	19.9	39.7	40.8	18.7	740.0	1.7
Vermont	Montpelier	1,065	103.5	10.3	4.4	3.0	9.6	53.2	1.9
Virginia	Richmond	25,399	1,891.9	13.4	77.0	50.0	12.6	0.0	
Washington	Olympia	9,234	457.1	20.2	11.4	12.0	19.2	116.2	3.9
West Virginia	Charleston	28,306	1,934.0	14.6	83.9	64.0	13.6	323.5	6.0
Wisconsin	Madison	24,913	1,992.3	12.5	41.8	48.5	12.0	477.5	4.2
Wyoming	Cheyenne	13,344	876.4	15.2	28.8	10.0	14.6	210.6	4.2

Table B-2. Data for School Districts Serving Capital Cities – Sorted by Student-to-Teacher Ratio
Source: National Center for Education Statistics, Common Core of Data, 2003-2004
Median Student-to-Teacher Ratio: 15.2/1

State	Capital	Students	Teachers	Students Per Teacher	Counselors	Library/Media Specialist	Students Per Teacher, Counselor, &Library/Media Specialist	Instructional Aides	Teachers Per Instructional Aide
Vermont	Montpelier	1,065	103.5	10.3	4.4	3.0	9.6	53.2	1.9
Maine	Augusta	2,611	244.7	10.7	10.0	2.0	10.2	99.1	2.5
Wisconsin	Madison	24,913	1,992.3	12.5	41.8	48.5	12.0	477.5	4.2
New York	Albany	9,919	787.4	12.6	14.5	14.6	12.1	269.0	2.9
New Jersey	Trenton	13,227	1,017.0	13.0	44.0	18.0	12.3	222.0	4.6
Connecticut	Hartford	22,578	1,717.4	13.1	42.0	37.0	12.6	426.0	4.0
Kansas	Topeka	14,049	1,071.4	13.1	35.5	31.5	12.3	345.1	3.1
Iowa	Des Moines	31,086	2,328.5	13.4	88.5	21.0	12.8	534.8	4.4
Pennsylvania	Harrisburg	7,883	587.0	13.4	24.0	6.0	12.8	79.0	7.4
Virginia	Richmond	25,399	1,891.9	13.4	77.0	50.0	12.6	0.0	
South Carolina	Columbia	26,990	1,986.8	13.6	87.0	54.0	12.7	448.0	4.4
Nebraska	Lincoln	32,120	2,341.6	13.7	69.9	50.8	13.0	388.4	6.0
Georgia	Atlanta	52,103	3,692.0	14.1	133.0	92.0	13.3	738.0	5.0
Tennessee	Nashville	68,651	4,857.6	14.1	180.5	119.0	13.3	711.0	6.8
Delaware	Dover	5,909	416.4	14.2	15.0	6.0	13.5	79.1	5.3
Indiana	Indianapolis	39,989	2,769.8	14.4	67.3	46.9	13.9	532.9	5.2
Missouri	Jefferson City	8,228	570.3	14.4	30.0	16.0	13.4	134.0	4.3
New Mexico	Albuquerque	90,537	6,191.0	14.6	206.2	93.5	13.9	1,532.5	4.0
West Virginia	Charleston	28,306	1,934.0	14.6	83.9	64.0	13.6	323.5	6.0
Arkansas	Little Rock	25,346	1,726.0	14.7	77.0	49.0	13.7	374.0	4.6
Texas	Austin	79,007	5,354.4	14.8	162.1	98.9	14.1	747.0	7.2
Louisiana	Baton Rouge	46,644	3,137.0	14.9	312.0	97.0	13.2	641.0	4.9
Alabama	Montgomery	32,553	2,171.5	15.0	71.0	59.0	14.1	263.5	8.2
North Carolina	Raleigh	109,424	7,302.0	15.0	260.0	168.0	14.2	1,727.0	4.2
Wyoming	**Cheyenne**	**13,344**	**876.4**	**15.2**	**28.8**	**10.0**	**14.6**	**210.6**	**4.2**
Massachusetts	Boston	60,150	3,926.3	15.3	229.8	20.5	14.4	787.8	5.0
Minnesota	St. Paul	42,510	2,754.0	15.4	81.4	45.4	14.8	1,195.4	2.3
Rhode Island	Providence	27,900	1,779.0	15.7			15.7		
North Dakota	Bismarck	10,477	662.1	15.8	25.1	12.4	15.0	158.0	4.2
Illinois	Springfield	15,212	944.7	16.1	0.0	7.0	16.0	0.0	
New Hampshire	Concord	5,473	339.9	16.1	17.8	5.3	15.1	150.8	2.3
Ohio	Columbus	63,098	3,838.4	16.4	126.8	70.8	15.6	1,096.3	3.5
Hawaii	Honolulu	183,609	11,128.5	16.5	674.5	290.0	15.2	2,639.7	4.2
Kentucky	Frankfort	6,026	365.1	16.5	10.0	9.5	15.7	121.3	3.0
South Dakota	Pierre	2,670	162.0	16.5	8.0	1.0	15.6	82.4	2.0

Table B-2. Continued.

State	Capital	Students	Teachers	Students Per Teacher	Coun-selors	Library/Media Specialist	Students Per Teacher, Counselor, &Library/Media Specialist	Instructional Aides	Teachers Per Instructional Aide
Maryland	Annapolis	74,508	4,501.1	16.6	-96.1	107.8	15.5	625.9	7.2
Mississippi	Jackson	31,640	1,900.8	16.6	88.2	63.2	15.4	532.6	3.6
Colorado	Denver	72,100	4,217.8	17.1	59.3	109.0	16.4	1,118.7	3.8
Nevada	Carson City	8,798	507.7	17.3	17.0	9.0	16.5	145.4	3.5
Oklahoma	Oklahoma City	40,599	2,344.9	17.3	33.3	49.0	16.7	456.3	5.1
Montana	Helena	8,084	465.0	17.4	11.5	13.8	16.5	50.8	9.2
Florida	Tallahassee	32,194	1,817.0	17.7	72.0	41.0	16.7	606.0	3.0
Idaho	Boise	26,211	1,466.2	17.9	77.5	11.2	16.9	252.3	5.8
Alaska	Juneau	5,475	305.0	18.0	-1.5	3.0	17.1	106.5	2.9
Arizona	Phoenix	34,884	1,788.1	19.5	38.0	34.1	18.8	381.4	4.7
California	Sacramento	52,103	2,659.0	19.6	22.9	13.8	19.3	309.5	8.6
Utah	Salt Lake City	24,443	1,229.7	19.9	59.7	40.8	18.7	740.0	1.7
Washington	Olympia	9,234	457.1	20.2	11.4	12.0	19.2	116.2	3.9
Oregon	Salem	37,785	1,772.5	21.3	50.7	49.9	19.8	635.4	2.8
Michigan	Lansing	16,979							

Table B-3. Data for School Districts Serving Capital Cities – Sorted by Student-to-Teacher Ratio With Teachers Including Counselors and Library/Media Specialists

Source: National Center for Education Statistics, Common Core of Data, 2003-2004

Median Student-to-Teacher, Counselor, and Library Media Specialist Ratio: 14.4/1

State	Capital	Students	Teachers	Students Per Teacher	Coun- selors	Library/ Media Specialist	Students Per Teacher, Counselor, &Library/Media Specialist	Instructional Aides	Teachers Per Instr. Aide
Vermont	Montpelier	1,065	103.5	10.3	4.4	3.0	9.6	53.2	1.9
Maine	Augusta	2,611	244.7	10.7	10.0	2.0	10.2	99.1	2.5
Wisconsin	Madison	24,913	1,992.3	12.5	41.8	48.5	12.0	477.5	4.2
New York	Albany	9,919	787.4	12.6	14.5	14.6	12.1	269.0	2.9
New Jersey	Trenton	13,227	1,017.0	13.0	44.0	18.0	12.3	222.0	4.6
Kansas	Topeka	14,049	1,071.4	13.1	35.5	31.5	12.3	345.1	3.1
Connecticut	Hartford	22,578	1,717.4	13.1	42.0	37.0	12.6	426.0	4.0
Virginia	Richmond	25,399	1,891.9	13.4	77.0	50.0	12.6	0.0	
South Carolina	Columbia	26,990	1,986.8	13.6	87.0	54.0	12.7	448.0	4.4
Iowa	Des Moines	31,086	2,328.5	13.4	88.5	21.0	12.8	534.8	4.4
Pennsylvania	Harrisburg	7,883	587.0	13.4	24.0	6.0	12.8	79.0	7.4
Nebraska	Lincoln	32,120	2,341.6	13.7	69.9	50.8	13.0	388.4	6.0
Louisiana	Baton Rouge	46,644	3,137.0	14.9	312.0	97.0	13.2	641.0	4.9
Georgia	Atlanta	52,103	3,692.0	14.1	133.0	92.0	13.3	738.0	5.0
Tennessee	Nashville	68,651	4,857.6	14.1	180.5	119.0	13.3	711.0	6.8
Missouri	Jefferson City	8,228	570.3	14.4	30.0	16.0	13.4	134.0	4.3
Delaware	Dover	5,909	416.4	14.2	15.0	6.0	13.5	79.1	5.3
West Virginia	Charleston	28,306	1,934.0	14.6	83.9	64.0	13.6	323.5	6.0
Arkansas	Little Rock	25,346	1,726.0	14.7	77.0	49.0	13.7	374.0	4.6
Indiana	Indianapolis	39,989	2,769.8	14.4	67.3	46.9	13.9	532.9	5.2
New Mexico	Albuquerque	90,537	6,191.0	14.6	206.2	93.5	13.9	1,532.5	4.0
Texas	Austin	79,007	5,354.4	14.8	162.1	98.9	14.1	747.0	7.2
Alabama	Montgomery	32,553	2,171.5	15.0	71.0	59.0	14.1	263.5	8.2
North Carolina	Raleigh	109,424	7,302.0	15.0	260.0	168.0	14.2	1,727.0	4.2
Massachusetts	**Boston**	**60,150**	**3,926.3**	**15.3**	**229.8**	**20.5**	**14.4**	**787.8**	**5.0**
Wyoming	Cheyenne	13,344	876.4	15.2	28.8	10.0	14.6	210.6	4.2
Minnesota	St. Paul	42,510	2,754.0	15.4	81.4	45.4	14.8	1,195.4	2.3
North Dakota	Bismarck	10,477	662.1	15.8	25.1	12.4	15.0	158.0	4.2
New Hampshire	Concord	5,473	339.9	16.1	17.8	5.3	15.1	150.8	2.3
Hawaii	Honolulu	183,609	11,128.5	16.5	674.5	290.0	15.2	2,639.7	4.2
Mississippi	Jackson	31,640	1,900.8	16.6	88.2	63.2	15.4	532.6	3.6

Table B-3. Continued.

State	Capital	Students	Teachers	Students Per Teacher	Coun-selors	Library/ Media Specialist	Students Per Teacher, Counselor, &Library/Media Specialist	Instructional Aides	Teachers Per Instr. Aide
Maryland	Annapolis	74,508	4,501.1	16.6	196.1	107.8	15.5	625.9	7.2
South Dakota	Pierre	2,670	162.0	16.5	8.0	1.0	15.6	82.4	2.0
Ohio	Columbus	63,098	3,838.4	16.4	126.8	70.8	15.6	1,096.3	3.5
Kentucky	Frankfort	6,026	365.1	16.5	10.0	9.5	15.7	121.3	3.0
Rhode Island	Providence	27,900	1,779.0	15.7			15.7		
Illinois	Springfield	15,212	944.7	16.1	0.0	7.0	16.0	0.0	
Colorado	Denver	72,100	4,217.8	17.1	69.3	109.0	16.4	1,118.7	3.8
Nevada	Carson City	8,798	507.7	17.3	17.0	9.0	16.5	145.4	3.5
Montana	Helena	8,084	465.0	17.4	11.5	13.8	16.5	50.8	9.2
Florida	Tallahassee	32,194	1,817.0	17.7	72.0	41.0	16.7	606.0	3.0
Oklahoma	Oklahoma City	40,599	2,344.9	17.3	33.3	49.0	16.7	456.3	5.1
Idaho	Boise	26,211	1,466.2	17.9	77.5	11.2	16.9	252.3	5.8
Alaska	Juneau	5,475	305.0	18.0	11.5	3.0	17.1	106.5	2.9
Utah	Salt Lake City	24,443	1,229.7	19.9	39.7	40.8	18.7	740.0	1.7
Arizona	Phoenix	34,884	1,788.1	19.5	33.0	34.1	18.8	381.4	4.7
Washington	Olympia	9,234	457.1	20.2	11.4	12.0	19.2	116.2	3.9
California	Sacramento	52,103	2,659.0	19.6	22.9	13.8	19.3	309.5	8.6
Oregon	Salem	37,785	1,772.5	21.3	90.7	49.9	19.8	635.4	2.8
Michigan	Lansing	16,979							

Table B-4. Data for School Districts Serving Capital Cities – Sorted by Teacher-to-
        Instructional Aide Ratio
        Source: National Center for Education Statistics, Common Core of Data, 2003-
        2004
        Median Teacher-to-Instructional Aide Ratio: 4.2/1

State	Capital	Students	Teachers	Instructional. Aides	Teachers/ Instructional Aide
Utah	Salt Lake City	24,443	1,229.7	740.0	1.7
Vermont	Montpelier	1,065	103.5	53.2	1.9
South Dakota	Pierre	2,670	162.0	82.4	2.0
New Hampshire	Concord	5,473	339.9	150.8	2.3
Minnesota	St. Paul	42,510	2,754.0	1,195.4	2.3
Maine	Augusta	2,611	244.7	99.1	2.5
Oregon	Salem	37,785	1,772.5	635.4	2.8
Alaska	Juneau	5,475	305.0	106.5	2.9
New York	Albany	9,919	787.4	269.0	2.9
Florida	Tallahassee	32,194	1,817.0	606.0	3.0
Kentucky	Frankfort	6,026	365.1	121.3	3.0
Kansas	Topeka	14,049	1,071.4	345.1	3.1
Nevada	Carson City	8,798	507.7	145.4	3.5
Ohio	Columbus	63,098	3,838.4	1,096.3	3.5
Mississippi	Jackson	31,640	1,900.8	532.6	3.6
Colorado	Denver	72,100	4,217.8	1,118.7	3.8
Washington	Olympia	9,234	457.1	116.2	3.9
Connecticut	Hartford	22,578	1,717.4	426.0	4.0
New Mexico	Albuquerque	90,537	6,191.0	1,532.5	4.0
Wyoming	Cheyenne	13,344	876.4	210.6	4.2
Wisconsin	Madison	24,913	1,992.3	477.5	4.2
North Dakota	Bismarck	10,477	662.1	158.0	4.2
Hawaii	Honolulu	183,609	11,128.5	2,639.7	4.2
North Carolina	**Raleigh**	**109,424**	**7,302.0**	**1,727.0**	**4.2**
Missouri	Jefferson City	8,228	570.3	134.0	4.3
Iowa	Des Moines	31,086	2,328.5	534.8	4.4
South Carolina	Columbia	26,990	1,986.8	448.0	4.4
New Jersey	Trenton	13,227	1,017.0	222.0	4.6
Arkansas	Little Rock	25,346	1,726.0	374.0	4.6
Arizona	Phoenix	34,884	1,788.1	381.4	4.7
Louisiana	Baton Rouge	46,644	3,137.0	641.0	4.9
Massachusetts	Boston	60,150	3,926.3	787.8	5.0
Georgia	Atlanta	52,103	3,692.0	738.0	5.0
Oklahoma	Oklahoma City	40,599	2,344.9	456.3	5.1
Indiana	Indianapolis	39,989	2,769.8	532.9	5.2
Delaware	Dover	5,909	416.4	79.1	5.3
Idaho	Boise	26,211	1,466.2	252.3	5.8
West Virginia	Charleston	28,306	1,934.0	323.5	6.0
Nebraska	Lincoln	32,120	2,341.6	388.4	6.0
Tennessee	Nashville	68,651	4,857.6	711.0	6.8
Texas	Austin	79,007	5,354.4	747.0	7.2
Maryland	Annapolis	74,508	4,501.1	625.9	7.2
Pennsylvania	Harrisburg	7,883	587.0	79.0	7.4
Alabama	Montgomery	32,553	2,171.5	263.5	8.2
California	Sacramento	52,103	2,659.0	309.5	8.6
Montana	Helena	8,084	465.0	50.8	9.2
Virginia	Richmond	25,399	1,891.9	0.0	
Rhode Island	Providence	27,900	1,779.0	N/A	
Illinois	Springfield	15,212	944.7	N/A	
Michigan	Lansing	16,979			

Appendix C

Redesigning Real Schools

The real schools used to illustrate redesigned schools were selected from school districts that serve capital cities of states in the United States. The selection criteria were district and school student-to-teacher ratio and school grade organization that are considerably different from the Columbia School District illustration in Chapter 1. The intent is to show that redesigning schools along the lines recommended in this book can be applied in a variety of school situations. Data for districts and schools is taken from the National Center for Education Statistics Common Core of Data for the 2003-2004 school year. The real names of the districts and schools are not used. For each illustration, three schools are presented; an elementary school, a middle level school, and a high school.

It was necessary to make some assumptions regarding the number of counselors, library/ media specialists, nurses, and instructional aides assigned to schools because these data are not given for individual schools. The assumptions are the following:

- The number of counselors for schools is varied between one for every 300 to 500 students depending on the number of counselors at the elementary and secondary level in the district.
- One library/media specialist is assigned to each school unless the data showed that there were not enough library/media specialists in the district for each school to have a fulltime person. In such cases, library/media specialists were omitted for the elementary school.
- One nurse was assigned to each school unless the data showed a relatively small number of Student Support Service Staff. When the number of Student Support Services Staff was low, nurses were omitted at the elementary school.
- The number of instructional aides was determined by applying the ratio of teachers-to-instructional aides for the district to the number of teachers in the school.

It is necessary to subtract pre-kindergarten and kindergarten teachers from the total number of teachers for elementary schools. Because theses data were not given by school, we assumed half-day kindergarten with student-to-teacher ratios between 30 and 40.

Adams Public Schools

The Adams Public Schools reported the following data to NCES for the 2003-2004 school year:

- Number of schools   32
- Enrollment   14,049
- FTE Classroom teachers   1,071.4
- Student-to-teacher ratio   13.1
- Elementary counselors   12.0
- Secondary counselors   23.5
- Library/media specialists   35.1
- Instructional aides   345.1
- Teachers-to-instructional aide ratio   3.1
- Student support services   168.7

The typical elementary school in the Adams School District has grades kindergarten through 5; middle school, grades 6 through 8; and high school, grades 9 through 12. This school district and schools were selected primarily because of the relatively low student-to-teacher ratio and the grade organization of the schools.

It is assumed that world languages are only offered at the high school.

An elementary, middle school, and high school were selected for illustrations. The data for the three schools are given in Figure C-1. Student, teacher, and grade organizations are actual data. The rest of the data are based on the assumptions we made about the various factors.

Figure C-1. Data for the Three Schools in the Adams School District

Schools →	Adams Elementary School					Adams Middle School			Adams High School			
Grades	1	2	3	4	5	6	7	8	9	10	11	12
Students	50	56	44	40	49	188	164	198	324	270	240	219
Students	241					550			1053			
Teachers	24					44			65			
Counselors	0					2			3			
Lib./Media Spec*	1					1			1			
Nurse	0					1			1			
Instr Aides*	8					15			23			
Students/Teacher	9.6					11.4			16.2			

* Lib./Media Spec. = library/media specialist, Instr. Aides = instructional aides

Adams Elementary School

Figure C-2 gives the staffing for the seven teaching teams at Adams Elementary School. In the case of this "two section" elementary school, each Academic Team has two regular teachers and one special education teacher assigned to the team. The regular teachers are listed in the chart as half time to a specific subject area specialty. This is arbitrary. In reality, the team would make decisions about specialization.

Figure C-3 gives the basic schedule for Adams Elementary School. The maximum number of students that the ten PDM and FA/T teachers work with at a time is 150 for an average group size of 15.0.

Note that the Academic Teams for grades 1, 2, and 3 have the same preparation time, and the Academic Teams for grades 4 and 5 have the same preparation time. This provides opportunity for collaboration among teachers with the same subject area specialization and for special education teachers to consult with colleagues who have different categorical certification/expertise.

Figure C-2. Adams Central Elementary School – Teaching Teams

Academic Grade 1 50 students	Academic Grade 2 56 students	Academic Grade 3 44 students	Academic Grade 4 40 students	Academic Grade 5 49 students	PDM Grades 1-5 241 students	Art/Tech. Grades 1-5 241 students
Teachers with Subject Area/Instructional Specialization						
.5 Lang. Arts* .5 Mathematics .5 Science .5 Soc. Studies* Special Ed.	.5 Lang. Arts .5 Mathematics .5 Science .5 Soc. Studies Special Ed.	.5 Lang. Arts .5 Mathematics .5 Science .5 Soc. Studies Special Ed.	.5 Lang. Arts .5 Mathematics .5 Science .5 Soc. Studies Special Ed.	.5 Lang. Arts .5 Mathematics .5 Science .5 Soc. Studies Special Ed.	Hlth./Phys. Ed.* Hlth./Phys. Ed. Hlth./Phys. Ed. F&C Science Special Ed.	Visual Art Music Technology Lib./Media * Special Ed.
Student-to-Teachers Ratios						
3 FTE teachers S/T = 16.7	3 FTE teachers S/T = 18.7	3 FTE teachers S/T = 14.7	3 FTE teachers S/T = 13.3	3 FTE teachers. S/T = 16.3	5 FTE teachers S/T = 48.2 10 FTE teachers S/T = 24.1	5 FTE teachers S/T = 48.2
Paraprofessionals						
Instr. Aide	Instr. Aide	Instr. Aide	Instr. Aide	Instr. Aide	.5 Instr. Aide Health Aide	.5 Instr. Aide Media Aide

* Lang. Arts = Language Arts, Soc. Studies = Social Studies, Special Ed. = Special Education, Hlth./Phys. Ed. = Health/ Physical Education, F&C Science = Family and Consumer Science, Lib./Meida = library/media specialist, FTE = fulltime equivalent, Instr. Aide = instructional aide.

Figure C-3. Basic Schedule for a Typical School Day for Adams Elementary School

Periods	Grade 1	Grade 2	Grade 3	Grade 4	Grade 5
Students	50	56	44	40	49
1	Academic	Academic	Academic	PDM – FA/T	PDM–FA/T
2					
3				Academic	Academic
4					
5	PDM – FA/T	PDM – FA/T	PDM – FA/T		
6					

Academic Teams for Grades 1, 2, and 3 have preparation time during Periods 5 and 6. Academic Teams for Grades 4 and 5 have preparation time during Periods 1 and 2. PDM and FA/T Teams have preparation time during Periods 3 and 4.

Adams Middle School

Figure C-4 gives the staffing for the five teaching teams at Adams Middle School. In this case, for the three Academic Teams, there are two teachers with specialization in each of the four subject areas.

Figure C-4. Adams Middle School – Teaching Teams

Academic – 6 188 students	Academic – 7 164 students	Academic – 8 198 students	PDM 550 students	FA/T 550 students
Teachers with Subject Areas/Instructional Specialization				
Language Arts* Language Arts Mathematics Mathematics Science Science Social Studies Social Studies Special Education Special Education	Language Arts Language Arts Mathematics Mathematics Science Science Social Studies Social Studies Special Education Special Education	Language Arts Language Arts Mathematics Mathematics Science Science Social Studies Social Studies Special Education Special Education	Health/Phys. Ed. Health/Phys. Ed. Health/Phys. Ed. F&C Science F&C Science Counselor Counselor Nurse Special. Education	Visual Art Visual Art Music Music Technology Technology Lib./Media Special Education Special Education
Student-to-Teachers Ratios				
10 FTE* teachers S/T = 18.8	10 FTE teachers S/T = 16.4	10 FTE teachers S/T = 19.8	9 FTE teachers S/T = 61.1	9 FTE teachers S/T =61.1
			18 FTE teachers S/T = 30.1	
Paraprofessionals				
Instructional Aide Instructional Aide .33 Instructional Aide	Instructional Aide Instructional Aide .33 Instructional Aide	Instructional Aide Instructional Aide .34 Instructional. Aide	Health Aide Counselor Aide Instructional Aide Instructional Aide	Media Aide Instructional Aide Instructional Aide Instructional Aide

Figure C-5 gives the basic schedule for a typical school day at Adams Middle School. The maximum number of students that the 18 PDM and FA/T teachers work with at a time is 352 for an average group size of 19.6.

Figure C-5. Basic Schedule for a Typical School Day for Adams Middle School

Periods	Grade 6	Grade 7	Grade 8
Students	188	164	198
1	PDM – FA/T	PDM –FA/T	Academic
2			
3	Academic	Academic	
4			
5			PDM – FA/T
6			
Academic Teams for Grades 6 and 7 have preparation time during Periods 1 and 2. The Academic Team for Grade 8 has preparation time during Periods 5 and 6. PDM and FA/T Teams have preparation time during Periods 3 and 4.			

Adams High School

Figure C-6 gives the staffing for six teaching teams at Adams High School. In this case with considerable variability in the number of students in each grade level, the 9th grade Academic Team has three teachers with specialty in each of the four subject areas while the 10th grade team has FTE of 2.5 in each of the four subject areas and the 11th and 12 grade have two teachers with specialization in each of the four subject areas.

Figure C-6. Adams High School – Teaching Teams

Academic Grade 9 324 students	Academic Grade 10 270 students	Academic Grade 11 240 students	Academic Grade 12 219 students	PDM 1053 students	FA/T/WL 1053 students
Teachers with Subject Area/Instructional Specialization					
Language Arts	Language Arts	Language Arts	Language Arts	Health/Phys. Ed.	Visual Art
Language Arts	Language Arts	Language Arts	Language Arts	Health/Phys. Ed.	Visual Art
Language Arts	Language Arts	Mathematics	Mathematics	Health/Phys. Ed.	Music
Mathematics	Mathematics	Mathematics	Mathematics	Health/Phys. Ed.	Music
Mathematics	Mathematics	Science	Science	F&C Science	Technology
Mathematics	Mathematics	Science	Science	F&C Science	Technology
Science	Science	Social Studies	Social Studies	F&C Science	Technology
Science	Science	Social Studies	Social Studies	Counselor	World Language
Science	Science			Counselor	World Language
Social Studies	Social Studies			Counselor	World Language
Social Studies	Social Studies			Nurse	Library/Media
Social Studies	Soc. Studies				
Special Education	Special Education.	Special Education.	Special Education	Special Education	Special Education
Special Education	Special Education.				
14 FTE teachers S/T = 23.1	14 FTE teachers S/T = 19.3	9 FTE teachers S/T = 26.7	9 FTE teachers S/T = 24.3	12 FTE teachers S/T = 87.7	12 FTE teachers S/T = 87.7
				24 FTE teachers S/T = 43.9	
Paraprofessionals					
Instructional Aide	Instructional Aide	Instructional Aide	Instructional Aide	Health Aide	Media Aide
Instructional Aide	Instructional Aide	Instructional Aide	Instructional Aide	Counselor Aide	Media Aide
Instructional Aide	Instructional Aide	Instructional Aide	Instructional Aide	Instructional Aide	Instructional Aide
				Instructional Aide	Instructional Aide
				Instructional Aide	Instructional Aide
					Instructional Aide

Figure C-7 gives the basic schedule for a typical school day at Adams High School. The maximum number of students that the 24 PDM and FA/T/WL teachers work with at a time is 594 for an average group size of 24.7.

156

Figure C-7. Basic Schedule for a Typical School Day for Adams High School

Periods	Grade 9	Grade 10	Grade 11	Grade 12
	324	270	240	219
1	PDM – FA/T/WL	PDM –FA/T/WL	Academic	Academic
2				
3	Academic	Academic		
4				
5			PDM – FA/T/WL	PDM – FA/T/WL
6				

Academic Teams for Grades 9 and 10 have preparation time during Periods 1 and 2. Academic Teams for Grades 11 and 12 have preparation time during Periods 5 and 6. PDM and FA/T/WL Teams have preparation time during Periods 3 and 4.

Jefferson School District

This illustration of the redesign scheme is a difficult one. The student-teacher ratio is relatively high, so the teacher resource available will be working with large numbers of students.

The Jefferson School District reported the following data to NCES for the 2002-2003 school year:

- Number of schools   50
- Enrollment   34,884
- FTE Classroom teachers   1,788.1
- Student-teacher ratio   19.5
- Elementary counselors   13.0
- Secondary counselors   25.0
- Library/media specialists   34.1
- Instructional aides   381.4
- Teacher-to-instructional aides ratio 4.7
- Student support services   95.8

This school district and the three schools were selected primarily because of the relatively high district student-to-teacher ratio.

The typical elementary school in the Jefferson School District has grades pre-kindergarten or kindergarten through 6; middle school, grades 7 and 8; and high school, grades 9 through 12.

It is assumed that world languages are offered only at the high school.

An elementary, middle school, and high school were selected for illustrations that have relatively high student-to-teacher ratios. The data for the three schools are given in Figure C-8. Student, teacher, and grade organizations are actual data. The rest of the data are based on the assumptions we made about the various factors. Note that kindergarten students are not included. It is assumed that Jefferson Elementary School has two fulltime kindergarten teachers for the 63 kindergarten students enrolled. The teacher count from the NCES data was reduced by two.

Figure C-8. Data for the Three Schools in the Jefferson School District

Schools →	Jefferson Elementary School (K-6)						Jefferson Middle School		Jefferson High School			
Grades	1	2	3	4	5	6	7	8	9	10	11	12
Students	114	79	93	81	77	92	411	421	489	518	487	492
Students	541						832		1986			
Teachers	31						39		92			
Counselors	0						2		4			
Lib/Media	1						1		1			
Nurse	0						1		1			
Instr. Aides	7						9		21			
Student/Teacher	16.9						19.3		19.7			

Jefferson Elementary School

Figure C-9 gives the staffing for the eight teaching teams at Jefferson Elementary School. In this school, some teachers on Academic Teams have half-time assignments to subject areas. This is arbitrary. In reality, the team would decide on the quantity of specialization/expertise need for each subject area.

Figure C-10 gives the basic schedule for Jefferson Elementary School. The maximum number of students that the eight PDM and FA/T teachers work with at a time is 286 for an average group size of 35.8. This is a relatively large number. To assist with this relatively high average number of students, four of the school's seven instructional aides are assigned to these two teams.

Figure C-9. Jefferson Elementary School – Teaching Teams

Academic Grade 1 114 students	Academic Grade 2 79 students	Academic Grade 3 93 students	Academic Grade 4 81 students	Academic Grade 5 77 students	Academic Grade 6 92 students	PDM 541 studemts	FA/T 541 students
Teachers with Subject Area/Instructional Specialization							
Lang. Arts Mathematics .5 Science .5 Soc. St. Special Ed.	Lang. Arts Mathematics .5 Science .5 Soc. St. Special Ed.	Lang. Arts Mathematics .5 Science .5 Soc. St. Special Ed.	Lang. Arts Mathematics .5 Science .5 Soc. St. Special Ed.	Lang. Arts Mathematics .5 Science .5 Soc. St. Special Ed.	Lang. Arts Mathematics .5 Science .5 Soc. St. Special Ed.	Hlth./Phys. Ed. Hlth./Phys. Ed. F&C Science. Counselor	Visual Art Music Technology Lib./Media
Student-to-Teacher Ratios							
4 FTE tchrs. S/T = 28.5	4 FTE teachers S/T = 19.8	4 FTE teachers S/T = 22.8	4 FTE teachers S/T = 20.0	4 FTE teachers S/T = 19.3	4 FTE teachers S/T = 23.0	4 FTE teachers S/T = 170.0	4 FTE teachers S/T = 170.0
						8 FTE teachers S/T = 85.0	
Paraprofessionals							
.5 Instr. Aide	.5 Instr. Aide	.5 Instr. Aide	.5 Instr. Aide	.5 Instr. Aide	.5 Instr. Aide	Health Aide Instr. Aide	Media Aide Instr. Aide

Figure C-10. Basic Schedule for a Typical School Day for Jefferson Elementary School

Periods	Grade 1 114	Grade 2 79	Grade 3 93	Grade 4 81	Grade 5 77	Grade 6 92
1	Academic	Academic	Academic	PDM – FA/T	PDM –FA/T	PDM – FA/T
2						
3				Academic	Academic	Academic
4						
5	PDM – FA/T	PDM – FA/T	PDM – FA/T			
6						
Academic Teams for Grades 1, 2, and 3 have preparation time during Periods 5 and 6. Academic Teams for Grades 4, 5, and 6 have preparation time during Periods 1 and 2. PDM and FA/T Teams have preparation time during Periods 3 and 4.						

An option for Jefferson Elementary School is multi-age/grade grouping of students. Figure C-11 shows the make-up of the five teaching teams when the multi-age/grade grouping is applied by combining grades 1 and 2, 3 and 4, and 5 and 6.

Figure C-12 gives the basic schedule for Jefferson Elementary School with multi-age/grade grouping. The maximum number of students that the 11 PDM and FA/T teachers work with at a time is 343 for an average group size of 31.2.

Figure C-11. Jefferson Elementary School – Teaching Teams with Multi-Age/Grade Grouping

Academic Grades 1 - 2 193 students	Academic Grades 3 - 4 174 students	Academic Grades 5 - 6 169 students	PDM 680 students	FA/T 680 students
Teachers with Subject Area/Instructional Specialization				
Language Arts Language Arts Mathematics Mathematics Science Social Studies Special Education	Language Arts Language Arts Mathematics Mathematics Science Social Studies Special Education	Language Arts Language Arts Mathematics Mathematics Science Social Studies Special Education	Health/ Phys. Ed. Health/ Phys. Ed. F&C Science Counselor Special Education	Visual Art Visual Art Music Technology Lib./Media Special Education
Student-to-Teacher Ratios				
7 FTE teachers S/T = 27.6	7 FTE teachers S/T=24.9	7 FTE teachers S/T = 24.1	5 FTE teachers S/T = 136.0	6 FTE teachers S/T = 113.3
			11 FTE teachers S/T = 61.8	
Paraprofessionals				
Instructional Aide	Instructional Aide	Instructional Aide	Health Aide Instructional Aide	Media Aide Instructional Aide

Figure C-12. Basic Schedule for a Typical School Day for Jefferson Elementary School

Periods	Grade 1 - 2 193	Grades 3 - 4 174	Grade 5 - 6 169
1	Academic	PDM - FA/T	PDM - FA/T
2			
3		Academic	Academic
4			
5	PDM – FA/T		
6			

Jefferson Middle School

Figure C-13 gives the staffing for the four teaching teams at Jefferson Middle School. The two Academic Teams for grades 7 and 8 are relatively large with 14 teachers. These teams could be subdivided.

160

Figure C-13. Jefferson Middle School – Teaching Teams

Academic Grade 7 411 students	Academic Grade 8 421 students	PDM 832 students	FA/T 832 students
Teachers with Subject Area/Instructional Specialization			
Language Arts	Language Arts	Health/Physical Education	Visual Art
Language Arts	Language Arts	Health/Physical Education	Music
Language Arts	Language Arts	F&C Science	Music
Mathematics	Mathematics	F&C Science	Technology
Mathematics	Mathematics	Counselor	Technology
Mathematics	Mathematics	Counselor	Library./Media
Science	Science	Nurse	
Science	Science		
Science	Science		
Social Studies	Social Studies		
Social Studies	Social Studies		
Social Studies	Social Studies		
Special Education	Special Education	Special Education	Special Education
Special Education	Special Education		
Student-to-Teacher Ratios			
14 FTE teachers S/T = 29.4	14 FTE teachers S/T = 30.1	8 FTE teachers S/T = 104.0	7 FTE teachers S/T = 118.9
		15 FTE teachers S/T = 55.5	
Instructional Aide .5 Instructional Aide	Instructional Aide .5 Instructional Aide	Health Aide Counselor Aide Instructional Aide	Media Aide Instructional Aide Instructional Aide

Figure C-14 gives the basic schedule for a typical school day at Jefferson Middle School. The maximum number of students that the 15 PDM and FA/T teachers work with at a time is 421 for an average group size of 28.1. To assist the teachers in these two teams, six of the nine instructional aides are assigned to them.

Figure C-14. Basic Schedule for a Typical School Day for Jefferson Middle School

Periods	Grade 7 411 students	Grade 8 421 students
1	PDM – FA/T	Academic
2		
3	Academic	
4		
5		PDM – FA/T
6		

Jefferson High School

Figure C-15 gives the staffing for 12 teaching teams Jefferson High School. Two Academic Teaching Teams have been created for each grade level, A and B. For this school, two PDM Teams, A and B, and two FA/T/WL Teams, A and B, have been created.

Figure C-15. Jefferson High School – Teaching Teams

Academic Grade 9 489 students	Academic Grade 10 518 students	Academic Grade 11 487 students	Academic Grade 12 492 students	PDM 1986 students	FE/T/WL 1986 students
Teachers with Subject Area/Instructional Specialization					
A9 Team 245 students	A10 Team 259 students	A11 Team 244 students	A12 Team 246 students	A Team 994 students	A Team 994 students
Language Arts Language Arts Mathematics Mathematics Science Science Social Studies Social Studies Special Education	Language Arts Language. Arts Mathematics Mathematics Science Science Social Studies Social Studies Special Education	Language Arts Language Arts Mathematics Mathematics Science Science Social Studies Social Studies Special Education	Language Arts Language Arts Mathematics Mathematics Science Science Social Studies Social Studies Special Education	Health/Phys.Ed. .5 Health/Phys.Ed. F&C Science. .5 F&C Science. Counselor Counselor .5 Nurse .5 Special Education	Visual Art Visual Art Music .5 Music Technology .5 Technology World Language World Language .5 Lib./Media .5 Special Education
B9 Team 244 students	B10 Team 259 students	B11 Team 243 students	B12 Team 246 students	B Team 992 students	B Team 992 students
Language Arts Language Arts Mathematics Mathematics Science Science Social Studies Social Studies Special Education	Language Arts Language Arts Mathematics Mathematics Science Science Social Studies Social Studies Special Education	Language Arts Language Arts Mathematics Mathematics Science Science Social Studies Social Studies Special Education	Language Arts Language Arts Mathematics Mathematics Science Science Social Studies Social Studies Special Education	Health/Phys. Ed. .5 Health/Phys. Ed. F&C Science .5 F&C Science Counselor Counselor .5 Nurse .5 Special. Education	Visual Art Visual Art Music .5 Music Technology .5 Technology World Lang. World Lang. .5 Lib./Media .5 Special Education
Student-to-Teacher Ratios					
18 FTE teachers S/T = 27.2	18 FTE teachers S/T = 28.8	18 FTE teachers S/T = 27.1	18 FTE teachers S/T = 27.3	12 FTE teachers S/T = 165.5	16 FTE teachers S/T = 124.1
				28 FTE teachers S/T = 70.9	
Paraprofessionals					
Instr.. Aide Instr. Aide Instr. Aide	Instr. Aide Instr. Aide Instr. Aide	Instr. Aide Instr. Aide Instr. Aide	Instr. Aide Instr. Aide Instr. Aide	Health Aide Counselor Aide Instr. Aide Instr. Aide Instr. Aide	Media Aide Media Aide Instr. Aide Instr. Aide

Figure C-16 gives the basic schedule for a typical school day at Jefferson High School. This schedule has the two PDM Teams and the two FA/T/WL Teams with the same preparation time during periods 3 and 4. The two 9th Grade Academic Teams and the two 11th Grade Academic Teams have preparation time during periods 1 and 2, and the two 10th Grade Academic Teams and the two 12th Grade Academic Teams have their preparation time during periods 5 and 6.

Figure C-16. Basic Schedule for a Typical School Day for Jefferson High School

Periods	A9 245 students	B9 244 students	A10 259 students	B10 259 students	A11 245 students	B11 244 students	A12 246 students	B12 246 students
1	PDM- FA/T/WL	PDM- FA/T/WL	Academic	Academic	PDM- FA/T/WL	PDM- FA/T/WL	Academic	Academic
2								
3	Academic	Academic			Academic	Academic		
4								
5			PDM- FA/T/WL	PDM- FA/T/WL			PDM- FA/T/WL	PDM- FA/T/WL
6								

The maximum number of students that 14 PDM and FA/T/WL teachers work with at a time is 518 for an average group size of 37.0. To assist teachers on these two teams, nine of the school's 21 instructional aides are assigned to them.

When student-teacher ratios for the school approach 20 to 1, the average number of students per teacher becomes relatively large. Of course, for schools with relatively high student-teacher ratios, these averages are already relatively large.

Closing Comment

The fact is, as the examples of Adams and Jefferson School Districts show, that there are great disparities in student-teacher ratios in schools in America. We believe that the benefits of small learning communities and teacher collaboration are great enough to make the effort to redesign schools regardless of the current resource situation. There are other solutions to the problem of redesigning schools for small learning communities and teacher collaboration. Some are probably better than the one presented in this book. The challenge for leaders is to redesign schools keeping in mind that the redesigned school will be different and that a different set of compromises will need to be made.

Appendix D

A Case Study: Implementing
The One Page® Strategic Planning Model

Columbia School District

Introduction

The fictional Columbia School district was used in Chapter 1 as a relatively simple illustration of the organization of teachers, students, and time in the school day to show the organization of small learning communities. The purpose of this organizational redesign was to provide one-third of the school day for common preparation time for interdisciplinary teaching teams. Here, a more complete case study of the Columbia School District is used to give examples of aligned plans using The One Page® Plan concept for the Superintendent, Middle School Principal, Team Leader for the Personal Decision-Making Team, a Health and Physical Education Teacher, and one student.

Case Study – The Columbia School District

The Columbia School District is located in a suburb of a metropolitan area that has a population of 30,000 people. The population has a mixture of racial/ethnic background: 50% White, 20% Black, 5% Native American, 10% Asian, and 15% Hispanic. The community is considered "middle class," but family incomes range from $15,000 to $350,000. The schools provide free or reduced lunches to 20% of the students.

The Columbia School District enrolls 2,600 students, K-12, in three schools: Columbia Elementary School (grades Kindergarten to 4), Columbia Middle School (grades 5 to 8), and Columbia High School (grades 9 to 12). Each grade has an enrollment of 200 students with a mixture of racial/ethnic backgrounds similar to the community. Ten percent of the student population at each grade level is classified as "special education."

Figure D-1 gives the organizational Chart for the Columbia School District. This chart shows the line organization from the Board of Education to the Superintendent and his direct reports, two district administrators and three principals. The named positions, Superintendent, George Washington, and Middle School Principal, Ben Franklin, are those for which plans are illustrated.

Figure D-2 gives the organizational chart for Columbia Middle School. This chart shows the line organization from the Principal, Ben Franklin, to the assistant principal and six teaching team leaders. Again, the named positions (Principal, Ben Franklin; Personal Decision-Making Team Leader, Abigail Adams, a Counselor; and Health and Physical Education Teacher, John Q. Adams) are those for which One Page Plans are illustrated. An illustration of the One Page Plan for one student; 5th grade student Abe Lincoln, has also been included.

Figure D-1. Columbia School District Organizational Chart

Columbia School District
Organizational Chart

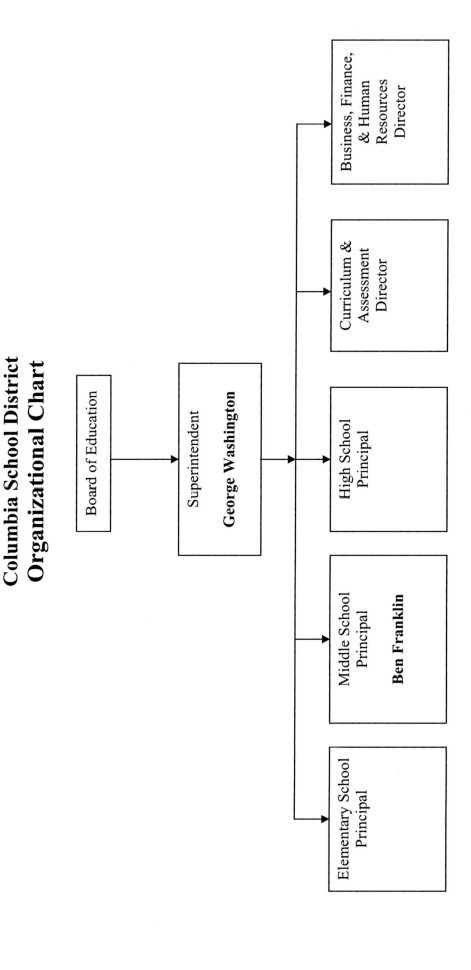

Figure D-2. Columbia Middle Level School Organizational Chart

Columbia Middle School
Organizational Chart

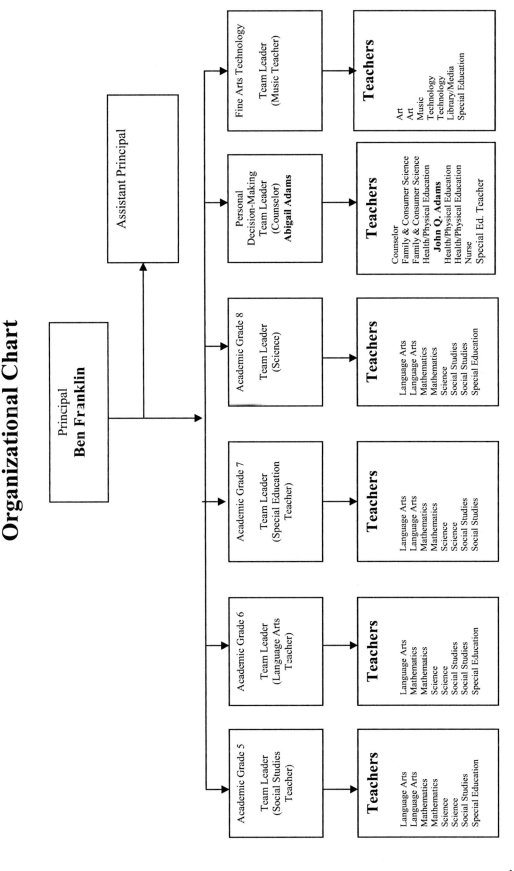

In the winter of 2007, the Columbia School District Board of Education approved the Superintendents recommendation to redesign the three schools in the district to form small learning communities and schedule one third of the school day (two hours of the six hour school day) for interdisciplinary teaching teams to work together collaboratively. The focus of teacher collaboration time is to be on improving curriculum, instruction, assessment, and professional practice using the processes of planning, development, implementation, and evaluation. The goal is improve student achievement in all subject areas and courses.

In addition to redesigning the organization of teachers, students, and time, curriculum is to be redesigned around ten subject areas and aligned with state or national content standards. A curriculum framework that provides enough detail to guide the development of instruction and assessment is to be used for all subject areas. An assessment framework, which provides for both external and internal assessments and ensures that data is available to teachers and teaching teams to frequently monitor student achievement, is to be applied to all courses in all subject areas.

The 2007-2008 school year is to be a transition year from the current design of instruction, curriculum, and assessment to the redesigned instruction, curriculum, and assessment. The school year will start with the current design and move to the redesign as teachers developed their knowledge and skill with respect to redesigning curriculum, instruction, and assessment.

Planning and preparation for the 2007-2008 school year began in the winter of 2007 and continued through the spring and summer prior to school starting in the fall. The results of that planning included the following:

- The One Page® Plans were written by the Superintendent and his direct reports, two district administrators and three principals, for the 2007-2008 year beginning July 1, 2007.

168

- The Board of Education adopted policies, recommended by the superintendent, supporting the redesign of instruction, curriculum, and assessment.

- Principals organized teachers into interdisciplinary teams and appointed team leaders.

- Principals received training for "leading teacher collaboration."

- Assistant Principals and Teaching Team Leaders wrote plans using The One Page® Strategic Planning Model.

- The Director of Curriculum and Assessment conducted workshops with principals, teaching team leaders, and selected teachers in each subject area in the application of the Curriculum and Assessment Frameworks. This included drafting a philosophy, strands, program goals, scope outline, and scope and sequence grid for each subject area using state or national content standards.

- Arrangements were made for monthly coaching for the superintendent and principals during the 2007-2008 school year.

- Teacher training was scheduled throughout the 2007-2008 school year for (1) developing skills for teacher collaboration skills and team autonomy, (2) writing One Page Plans for teachers, (3) the application of the curriculum and assessment frameworks, (4) writing instructional units including the writing of learner outcomes, and (5) personalizing student programs (being a Personal Adult Advocate and using The One Page® Planning model for Personal Plans for Progress for students). These training and development activities were scheduled throughout the 2007-2008 school year using two days of pre-school workshop time, the professional development day each quarter (total of four days) and three of the ten hours per week of teacher preparation time. (With six hours per pre-school workshop and professional development day, a total of 144 hours, or the equivalent of 24 six-hour days during the 2007-2008 school year is used for professional development of teachers related to these five areas.)

- Principals scheduled their participation, and assistant principal participation, in "frequently monitoring student achievement" once a week with each team during the first semester, and bi-weekly during the second semester.

- The Superintendent scheduled reviews of One Page Plans with each of his direct reports monthly from July 1, 2007 to June 30, 2008.
- Each Principal scheduled monthly reviews of One Page Plans with the Assistant Principal and each Teaching Team Leader during the 2007-2008 school year.

With these completed tasks and scheduled activities, the 2007-2008 budget aligned with the redesign efforts, school bus routes established, new staff selected and hired (with the involvement of team leaders), new supplies and equipment on hand (or ordered), summer maintenance completed, etc., the Columbia School District is ready to start the 2007-2008 school year for students.

Figures D-3, D-4, D-5, D-6, and D-7 are illustrations of One Page Plans for the Superintendent, the Middle School Principal, the Middle School Personal Decision-Making Team Leader, a Middle School Health and Physical Education Teacher, and a Middle School Student, respectively.

Introduction to the Plans

The Columbia School District did not have performance standards for courses in the past. Therefore, the objective for student learning performance is set as *at least 75 percent of students* achieving the performance standard in each course. In the future, objectives for student achievement will be set for growth in the percent of students achieving the performance standards of courses.

Likewise, the Columbia School District did not *numerical* data for parent/community satisfaction with the schools or for teacher job satisfaction. Therefore, the percents of parents/community being satisfied with the schools and teachers satisfied with their jobs are set *at least 75 percent* for parent/community satisfaction and *at least 80 percent* for teacher job satisfaction. In the future, these objectives will be stated in terms of growth of percent.

Many readers will not be familiar with The One Page® Plan methodology. An important feature of The One Page® Plan methodology is brevity. It is critical that the five components fit on one page and be easy to reference as a guide for direction and work of the individual and as a tool for review of accomplishments and progress. Therefore, it is often necessary to use acronyms and abbreviation. "Insiders" in a school or district know, or quickly learn, the meaning and use of these acronyms and abbreviation. To help the reader with the One Page Plans that follow, each plan is presented on the left-hand page and notes for the plan are presented on the right-hand page. The notes for each plan include a list of acronyms and abbreviations; notes about selected parts of a plan; and a table that shows the alignment of Objectives, Strategies, and Action Plans.

George Washington, Superintendent   Last Updated: 05/01/2(

vision

By 2014 ALL students in the Columbia School District will be successful learners. We will accomplish this by building (personalized learning environment and program for each student, (2) a rigorous curriculum, (3)an assessment program frequently monitoring student progress and accountability, (4) research-based instructional strategies, and (5) a cultur collaboration and continuous improvement.

mission

Successful Learning for ALL Students

objectives

1. Achieve at least 75% of students meeting performance standards in 168 courses in grades 1-12 by June 2008.
2. Reduce high school dropout rate from 15.8% to 10.0% by June 2008.
3. Achieve at least 75% of parents/community satisfied with the schools by June 2008.
4. Achieve at least 80% of teachers highly satisfied with their jobs by June 2008.

strategies

1. Promote school redesign by revising policies creating One Page Plans for dir. rpts., & monitoring.
2. Monitor One Page Plan progress by mthly. admin. mtgs., mthly. 1-on-1s, bi-wkly. tours of each school.
3. Frequently monitor student ach. by mthly. review mtgs w/ prins., qtrly. rpts. to BOE, & updating IT Rpt. Sys.
4. Redesign curriculum by establishing a common framework, conducting wkshps. & monitoring development.
5. Redesign assessment by a common framework, summer wkshp, & monitoring development.
6. Promote parent/community sat. w/ schs. by mthly. newsletters, news releases, & reports to comm. orgs.
7. Monitor parent/community sat. w/ schs. by qrtrly. surveys, adv. cncl. mtgs., & fdbk. from comm. orgs.
8. Promote teacher job sat. by estb. teaching teams w/ autonomy, professional development, & recognition.
9. Monitor teacher job sat. by quarterly surveys, bi-wkly school visits, & meetings with principals.

action plans

1. Revise policies by July 31. (Supt.)
2. Write One Page Plans for direct reports by Aug. 31. (Supt.)
3. Conduct mthly. One Page Plan progress reviews w/ dir. rpts. Aug. thru Jun. (Supt.)
4. Conduct summer curriculum workshop by Aug. 10. (Dir. C/A/I)
5. Conduct summer assessment workshop by Aug. 20. (Dir. C/A/I)
6. Update IT reporting sys. by Nov. 30, 06. (Dir. C/A/I)
7. Report school programs & student progress & achievement July thru June. (Supt.)
8. Survey parent/community & tchr. job satisfaction by Nov. 15, Jan. 15, Apr. 15, and Jun 15. (Dir. C/A/I)
9. Survey teacher job satisfaction by Nov. 15, Jan.15, Apr. 15, and Jun 15. (Dir. C/A/I)

Figure D-3A. Columbia School District – Superintendent's One Page Plan – Notes

Abbreviations:

• C/A/I = Curriculum, Assessment, and Instruction • BOE = Board of Education • IT = Information Technology • dir. rprt. = direct reports • mthly = monthly • admin. = administration • mtg. = meeting • prin. = principal • cncl. = council • fdbk. = feedback	• estb. = establishing • qtrly. = quarterly • rpt. sys = reporting system • wkshp. = workshop • comm. = community • org. = organization • wkly = weekly • supt. = superintendent • dir. = director • tchr. = teacher

Notes for Strategies:

Strategy 1:
• The revised policies will require and support the instructional, curricular, and assessment practices that the Columbia School District wishes to implement. (See pages 6 and 7 for a listing.)
• The One Page® Plans will have vision and mission statements clearly focused on student learning.

Strategy 4:
• Redesign of the curriculum will be consistent with the common curriculum framework adopted by the board. (See page 89.)

Strategy 5:
• Redesign of assessment will be consistent with the common framework adopted by the board. (See page 131.)

Alignment of Strategies with Action Plans and Objectives within the Superintendent's Plan:

Strategy	Action Plan	Objective
1	1, 2, 3	1,2
2	3	1,2,3,4
3	3, 6	1,2
4	1, 2, 3, 4	1,2
5	1, 2, 3, 5, 6	1,2
6	7	3
7	8	3
8	1	4
9	9	4

Figure D-4. Columbia School District
Planning Unit: Columbia Middle School
School Year: 2007-2008

Ben Franklin, Principal   Last Updated: 5/22/2

vision

By 2011 ALL students at Columbia Middle School will be successfully prepared for the next step in their l
journey; which includes further learning in high school, family, and community service. We will accomp
this by building (1) a personalized learning environment and program, (2) a rigorous curriculum, (3)
assessment program for frequently monitoring student achievement, (4) researched-based instructic
strategies, and (5) a culture of collaboration and continuous improvement.

mission

Success for ALL Students

objectives

1. Achieve at least 75% of students meeting performance standards for the 56 CMS courses by June 2008.
2. Achieve at least 75% parent/community satisfaction with the Columbia Middle School by June 2008.
3. Achieve at least 80% of teachers with high job satisfaction at Columbia Middle School by June 2008.

strategies

1. Organize SLCs by establishing SWAS, common preparation time, TC, autonomy, & looping.
2. Develop TL & TC by leading mtgs., modeling ldr. beh., coaching, & monitoring team mtgs.
3. Create One Page Pans for TLs by presenting principal's plan, teaching one-page methodology, & coaching.
4. Monitor One Page Plan progress of TLs by bi-wkly. Sch. Ldrshp. Team mtgs. & mthly. 1-on-1s w/ TLs.
5. Develop curriculum by workshops, supervision, & monitoring.
6. Develop assessment programs by workshops, supervision, & frequently monitoring student achievement.
7. Inform parents/community thru mthly. newsletters, PTA mtgs, open house, & advisory council.
8. Monitor parent/community satisfaction by survey results, advisory council mtgs., & parent phone calls.
9. Monitor teacher job satisfaction by survey results, TL mtgs., monitoring team meetings, & wkly. clsrm tours.

action plans

1. Create Small Learning Communities by Jul. 1. (Principal)
2. Lead the development of Teacher Collaboration skills from Aug. 1 thru Oct. 31. (Principal)
3. Conduct bi-weekly Team Leader Meetings from Aug. thru Jun. (Principal)
4. Conduct monthly 1-on-1 mtgs. w/ TLs from Sept. thru Jun. (Principal)
5. Supervise teaching teams from Sept. through Jun. (Principal)
6. Write Team Leader One Page Plans by Sept. 30. (Principal)
7. Supervise the development of curriculum & assessment from Aug. thru May. (Principal)
8. Write monthly newsletters to parents/community from Aug. thru Jun. (Principal)
9. Monitor parent/community satisfaction with CMS by Nov. 15, Jan. 15, Apr. 15, & Jun. 15. (Principal)

Figure D-4A. Columbia Middle School –Principal's One Page Plan – Notes

Abbreviations:

• CMS = Columbia Middle School • SLC = small learning community • SWAS = school-within-a-school • TC = teacher collaboration • TL = team leader • mthly = monthly	• mtg. = meeting • wkshp. = workshop • wkly = weekly • tchr. = teacher • clsrm. = classroom

Notes for Strategies:

Strategy 1.
• Small learning communities also feature interdisciplinary teaching teams, differentiated staff, and a heterogeneous group of students. (See pages 26 through 44.)

Strategy 6:
• Curriculum will be consistent with the common curriculum framework adopted by the board. (See page 89.)

Strategy 7:
• Assessment development will be consistent with the common framework adopted by the board. (See page 131.)

Strategies 2,4,5, 6:
• In each of these strategies, the principal uses contingent rewards and recognition of group and individual accomplishments.

Alignment of Strategies with Action Plans and Objectives within the Principal's Plan

Strategy	Action Plan	Objective
1	1	1
2	2, 3, 4	1
3	6	1
4	3, 4	1
5	7	1
6	7	1
7	9	1
8	9	2
9	3, 4, 5, 7	3

Figure D-5. Columbia Middle School

Planning Unit: Personal Decision-Making Team
School Year: 2007-2008

Abigail Adams, Team Leader (Counselor)   Last Updated: 10/2/2

vision

By 2011 ALL 8th grade students at Columbia Middle School will be well prepared for their high school ye with respect to educational/career planning and development; personal, social, and family developm personal health and physical fitness; effective teenage stewards of financial resources; and wise teen consumers. We will accomplish this by working collaboratively to build effective decision- making skills individual student plans for progress through the middle school years.

mission

Creating Effective Decision-Makers

objectives

1.   Achieve at least 75% of students meeting performance standards in 12 CMS PDM courses by June 2008
2.   Achieve at least 80% parent/community satisfaction w/ PDM Program at CMS by June 2008.

strategies

1.   Frequently monitor student achievement by formative assessment, wkly. reviews, & problem solving.
2.   Report Assessment Results to teaching team, students, principal, & parents.
3.   Create One Page Plans for tchrs. by presenting TL plan, teaching one-page methodology, & coaching.
4.   Monitor One Page Plan progress of tchrs. by team meetings, & mthly. 1-on-1s w/ teachers.
5.   Provide Continuous Professional Development by assessing needs, PLP, & professional growth opportunities.
6.   Personalize students' ed. programs by PAA, PPP, involving families, & flexible scheduling/grouping.
7.   Develop curriculum & assessment by workshops, writing instructional units, & peer reviews with feedback.
8.   Monitor parent/community satisfaction w/ CMS PDM by survey, CMS Adv. Council, & parent feedback.
9.   Teach Guid. Cur. by using best tching. prac., collaborating w/ team members, & using assessment program.

action plans

1.   Conduct Team Meetings for FMSA, CD, and AD from Sept. thru Jun. (TL)
2.   Report student achievement/progress for PDM to principal from Oct. thru Jun. (TL)
3.   Write One Page Plans for team members by Nov 31. (TL)
4.   Conduct One Page Plan reviews monthly from Nov. thru June. (TL)
5.   Write One Page Plans for each student by Jan. 31. (PDM Teachers)
6.   Write Instructional Units from Nov. thru May. (PDM Teachers)
7.   Write Assessments from Nov. thru May. (PDM Teachers)
8.   Prepare materials for distribution to parents/community Aug. thru Jun. (TL)
9.   Teach Guidance Curriculum from Sept. thru Jun. (Counselor)

176

Figure D-5A. Columbia Middle School –Team Leader's One Page Plan – Notes

Abbreviations:

• CMS = Columbia Middle School • TC = teacher collaboration • TL = team leader • FMSA = frequently monitor student achievement • CD = curriculum development • AD = assessment development	• Guid. Cur. = Guidance Curriculum • tching. prac. = teaching practices • mthly = monthly • mtg. = meeting • wkshp. = workshop • wkly = weekly • tchr. = teacher

Notes for Objectives:

Objective 1:
- The 12 courses for the PDM in CMS are one course in each of the three subject areas (Health and Physical Education, Family and Consumer Science, and Guidance) over the four grades in CMS.

Notes for Strategies:

Strategy 6:
- PDM will take the lead in teaching teachers in the Academic Teams and the Fine Arts/Technology Team the concept of PAA and PPP for students and in introducing students to The One Page® Plan methodology. Teachers on other teams will become PAAs and work with students in the writing of their "one page plans."

Alignment of Strategies with Action Plans and Objectives within the Team Leader's Plan

Strategy	Action Plan	Objective
1	1	1
2	2	1
3	3	1
4	4	1
5	3, 5, 6, 7	1
6	5, 6, 7	1
7	6, 7	1
8	4	2
9	8	1

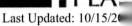

ON PAC PLA

John Q. Adams, Teacher   Last Updated: 10/15/2(

vision

By 2011 ALL 8th grade students at Columbia Middle School will choose to follow a health and fitness plan t is health-enhancing and risk-reducing. This will be accomplished by continuously engaging each student wi a rigorous Health and Physical Education curriculum that is personalized to the student's present and on-goi health and fitness status, using best teaching practices, and assessing progress toward health and fitness goal

mission

Building Healthy Bodies

objectives

1. Achieve at least 75% of students meeting the performance standards in 4 H/PE courses by June 2007.
2. Achieve at least 75% of parents/community satisfaction w/ the H/PE program at CMS by June 2007.

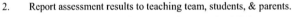

1. Frequently Monitor Student Achievement by formative assessments, wkly. reviews, & problem solving.
2. Report assessment results to teaching team, students, & parents.
3. Incorporate H/PE in students' PPPs by assessing H/PE status, setting H/PE goals, & teaching H/PE C&I.
4. Develop H/PE curriculum & assessment by wkshp., writing instructional units, & peer reviews w/ feedback.
5. Implement best H/PE teaching practices by professional development, writing instructional units, & teaching.

strategies

6. Communicate w/ parents by reporting assessment results, CMS website, e-mail, and phone calls.
7. Monitor parent/community satisfaction w/ H/PE by survey, CMS Advisory Council, & parent contacts.

1. Participate in Team Meetings for FMSA, CD, AD, & parent satisfaction from Nov. thru Jun. (Teacher)
2. Report student achievement/progress to students, parents, and PDM Team Oct. though Jun.. (Teacher)
3. Prepare One Page PPPs with students by Jan. 20. (Teacher)
4. Monitor One Page Plans of students from Jan. thru Jun. (Teacher)
5. Write Instructional Units from Sept. thru May. (Teacher)

action plans

6. Write H/PE Assessments from Sept. thru May. (Teacher)
7. Teach 4 H/PE courses from Sept. thru Jun. (Teacher)
8. Prepare materials for distribution to parents and community from Nov. thru Jun. (Teacher)

178

Figure D-6A. Columbia Middle School – H/PE Teacher's One Page Plan – Notes

Abbreviations:

• CMS = Columbia Middle School • FMSA = frequently monitor student ahievement • CD = curriculum development • AD = assessment development	• H/PE = Health and Physical Education • PPP – personal plan for progress • wkshp. = workshop

Alignment of Strategies with Action Plans and Objectives within the Team Leader's Plan

Strategy	Action Plan	Objective
1	1, 2, 4	1
2	2	1
3	3	1
4	5, 6	1
5	7	1
6	2, 8	2
7	1	2

The Personal Learning Plan

John Q. Adam's Personal Learning Plan is derived from the strategies and action plans which are part of The One Page® Plan that he wrote. The question is this: What are John's learning needs relative to the strategies and action plans? It is likely, for example, that John will need training with respect to the concept of Personal Plan for Progress and writing The One Page® Plans with students (Strategy 3, Action Plan 3) and developing curriculum and assessment using the district's frameworks (Strategy 4, Action Plans 5, 6). The steps of these action plans on the progress chart for John must include John's learning needs. In addition, problems with respect to using best teaching practices for H/PE may come up during the school year that may require John to acquire new knowledge and skill. If such problems arise, steps will need to be added to Action Plans 5 and/or 7.

Abe Lincoln, 5th grade student

vision

In four years, I will be prepared to enter High School by successfully meeting the performance standards for Middle School courses in which I enroll. I will accomplish this by regular school attendance, actively participating in classes, completing assignments on time, being courteous to students and adults, and workin with other students.

mission

Creating My Future

objectives

1. Achieve the 5th grade performance standards in the 9 5th grade subject area courses by June 2008.
2. Participate in 2 CMS extra-curricular activities during the school year.
3. Increase home study time to at least 1 hour on each of 5 days/wk. thruout the school year.

strategies

1. Complete work on time by an assignment log, using school time wisely, seeking help when needed.
2. Study by organizing materials, removing distractions, taking/reviewing notes, & practicing skills.
3. Participate in class by paying attention, taking/reviewing notes, asking questions, & offering comments.
4. Monitor progress & ach. by keeping a log of test results, determining improvement needs, & taking action
5. Select extra-curricular activities by considering my interests & abilities, time commitments, & schedule.

action plans

1. Establish a study area at home by Jan. 30. (Abe)
2. Organize a journal for assignments, achievement & progress charts, and calendar by Jan. 31. (Abe)
3. Report my learning progress and achievement to my family mthly. thruout the school year. (Abe)
4. Actively participate in classroom instruction in all courses thruout the school year. (Abe)
5. Complete assignments for all courses thruout the school year. (Abe)
6. Review notes from instruction & reading/viewing thruout the school year. (Abe)
7. Contribute to my study group's work thruout the school year. (Abe)
8. Participate in extra-curricular activities from Feb. thru May. (Abe)

D-7A. Columbia Middle School – 5th Grade Student's One Page Plan – Notes

Abbreviations:

• CMS = Columbia Middle School • PAA = personal adult advocate	• PPP = personal plan for progress • ach. = achievement

Alignment of Strategies with Action Plans and Objectives within the Team Leader's Plan

Strategy	Action Plan	Objective
1	2, 5	1,3
2	1, 4, 5, 6	1
3	4, 6	1
4	3	1
5	8	2

References

American Association of School Librarians and Association for Educational Communications and Technology. (1998). *Information power: Building partnerships for learning*. Chicago, Il: Author.

American School Counselor Association. (2005). *The ASCA national model: A framework for school counseling programs* (2nd ed.). Alexandria, VA: Author.

Blanchard, K., Randolph, A., & Grazier, P. (2005). *Go team! Take your team to the next level*. San Francisco: Berrett-Koehler Publishers, Inc.

Bloom, B. S. (Ed.). (1956). *Taxonomy of educational objectives: The classification of educational goals: Handbook I: Cognitive domain*. White Plains, New York: Longman.

Bloom, B. S, Hastings, J. T, & Madaus, G. F. (1971). *Handbook on formative and summative evaluation of student learning*. New York: McGraw-Hill.

Burney, D. (2004). Craft knowledge: The road to transforming schools. *Phi Delta Kappan, 85*, 526-531.

Bush, R. N. & Allen, D. W. (1964). *A new design for high school education*. New York: McGraw Hill.

Cawelti, G. (1997). *Effects of high school restructuring: Ten high schools at work*. Arlington, VA.: Educational Research Service.

Chrispeels, J. (2002). The California Center for Effective Schools: The Oxnard School District partnership. *Phi Delta Kappan, 83,* 382-387.

Cole, R.W. (Ed.) (1995). *Educating everybody's children: Diverse teaching strategies for diverse learners*. Alexandria, VA.: Association for Supervision and Curriculum Development.

Collins, J. (2001). *Good to great*. New York: Harper Collins Publishers, Inc.

Copeland, M. A. & Boatright, E. E. (2004). Leading small: Eight lessons for leaders in transforming large comprehensive high schools. *Phi Delta Kappan, 85*, 762-770.

Cotton, K. (2003). *Principals and student achievement: What the research says*. Alexandria, VA.: Association for Supervision and Curriculum Development.

Cotton, K. (2004). *New small learning communities: Findings of recent research.* Reston, VA.: National Association of Secondary School Principals.

Covey, S. R. (1989). *The 7 habits of highly effective people.* New York: Simon and Schuster, Inc.

Covey, S. R. (2004). *The 8th habit: From effectiveness to greatness.* New York: Simon and Schuster, Inc.

Covey, S. R. (Speaker). (2004). Compact Disc. *The 8th habit: From effectiveness to greatness.* New York: Simon and Schuster Audio Division, Simon and Schuster, Inc.

DuFour, R. (2005). What is a professional learning community? In R. DuFour, R. Eaker, and R. Dufour (Eds.), *On common ground: The power of professional learning communities* (31-43). Bloomington, IN.: National Education Service.

DuFour, R., DuFour, R., Eaker, R., and Many, T. (2006). *Learning by doing: A handbook for professional learning communities at work.* Bloomington, IN.: Solution Tree (formerly National Educational Service).

Edmonds, R. (1979). Effective schools for the urban poor. *Educational Leadership, 37,* 15-27.

English, F.W. & Larson, R. L. (1996). *Curriculum management for educational and social service organizations.* (2nd ed.). Springfield, IL.: Charles E. Thomas Publishers.

Evans, P. M. (2003). A principal's dilemmas: Theory and reality of school redesign. *Phi Delta Kappan, 84,* 424-437.

Fiore, D. J. (2004). *An Introduction to educational administration: Standards, theories, and practice.* Larchmont, NY.: Eye on Education.

Fullan, M. G. (2001). *The new meaning of educational change.* (3rd ed.). New York: Teachers College Press.

Fullan, M. (Speaker). (2005). *Systems thinkers in action.* (Cassette Recording No 505256). From ASCD's 60th Annual Conference, Orlando, Florida, April 2-4, 2005. Alexandria, VA.: Association for Supervision and Curriculum Development.

Gusky, T. (2005). Mapping the road to proficiency. *Educational Leadership, 63,* 32-38.

Hall, P. (2005). A school reclaims itself. *Educational Leadership, 62,* 70-73.

Hernandez-Murillo, R. & Roisman, D. (2004, April). Tough lesson: More money doesn't help schools; accountability does. *The Regional Economist,* 12-13.

Horan, J. (2004). *The One Page Business Plan®.* Berkeley, CA.: The One Page Business Plan® Company.

International Society for Technology in Education. (1998). *National educational technology standards for students.* Eugene, OR: Author

Jenkins, J. M. & Keefe, J. W. (2002). Two schools: Two approaches to personalized learning. *Phi Delta Kappan, 83,* 449-456.

Katzenbach, J. R. & Smith, D. K. (1993). *The wisdom of teams: Creating the high-performance organization.* New York: Harper Collins Publishers, Inc.

Keefe, J. W. and Jenkins, J. M. (2002). Personalized instruction. *Phi Delta Kappan, 83,* 440-448.

Krathwohl, D. R., Bloom, B. S., & Masia, B. B. (1964). *Taxonomy of educational objectives: The classification of educational goals: Handbook II: Affective domain.* White Plains, New York: Longman.

Leithwood, K., Louis, K., Anderson, S., & Wahlstrom, K. (2004). *How leadership influences student learning.* New York: The Wallace Foundation.

Levine, M. (2005). *Ready or not: Here life comes.* New York: Simon and Schuster.

Marzano, R. J. (2003). *What works in schools: Translating research into action.* Alexandria, VA.: Association for Supervision and Curriculum Development.

Marzano, R.J., Pickering, D. J., & Pollock, J. E. (2001). *Classroom instruction that works: Research-based strategies for increasing student achievement.* Alexandria, VA.: Association for Supervision and Curriculum Development.

Marzano, R. J., Waters, T., &McNulty, B. A. (2005). *School leadership that works: From research to results.* Alexandria, VA.: Association for Supervision and Curriculum Development.

Maurer, R. E. & Pedersen, S. C. (2004). *Malcolm and me: How to use the Baldridge process to improve your school.* Lanham, Md.: Scarecrow Education.

Meadors, D. (2005). Power, influence, and impact. *Camelback, 1*(6), 26-30.

Mid-continent Research for Education and Learning. (2005). *Participant's Manual for Balanced Leadership: School Leadership That Works™. Session 1 – Balanced Leadership Framework™: An Overview*. Aurora, CO.: Author.

National Association of School Nurses and American Nurses Association. (2005). *School nursing: Scope and standards of practice*. Silver Springs, MD.: Author

National Association of Secondary School Principals. (2004). *Breaking ranks II™: Strategies for leading high school reform*. Reston, VA.: Author

O'Shea, M. (2005). *From standards to success*. Alexandria, VA.: Association for Supervision and Curriculum Development.

Phi Delta Kappa. (2005). High school reform part one: The need. *Trends and Topics, 5*(4), 1.

Popham, J. (2005). Student attitudes count. *Educational Leadership, 62*, 84-85.

Ravitch, D. (2006) Commentary: National standards: '50 standards for 50 states' is a formula for incoherence and obfuscation. Retrieved January 6, 2006, from http://www.edweek.org/ew/articles/2006/01/05/17ravitch.h25.html

Reeves, D. (2002) *The daily disciplines of leadership*. San Francisco, CA.: John Wiley and Sons, Inc.

Reeves, D. (Speaker). (2005a). *The multiple intelligences of leadership: An alternative vision of leadership effectiveness*. (Cassette Recording No 505256). From ASCD's 60th Annual Conference, Orlando, Florida, April 2-4, 2005. Arlington, VA.: Association for Supervision and Curriculum Development.

Reeves, D. (2005b). Putting it all together: Standards, assessments, and accountability in successful professional learning community. In R. DuFour, R. Eaker, and R. Dufour (Eds.), *On common ground: The power of professional learning communities* (45-64). Bloomington, IN.: National Education Service.

Reeves, D. (2006). *The learning leader: How to focus school improvement for better results*. Alexandria, VA.: Association for Supervision and Curriculum Development.

Ruebling, C., Stow, S., Kayona, F., and Clarke, N. (2004). Instructional leadership: An essential ingredient for improving student learning. *The Educational Forum, 68*, 243-253.

Schmoker, M. (1999). *Results: The key to continuous school improvement.* (2nd ed.). Alexandria, VA.: Association for Supervision and Curriculum Development.

Schmoker, M. (2004). Tipping point: From Feckless reform to substantive instructional improvement. *Phi Delta Kappan, 85*, 424-432.

Schmoker, M. (2005). No turning back: The ironclad case for professional learning community. In R. DuFour, R. Eaker, and R. Dufour (Eds.), *On common ground: The power of professional learning communities* (135-153). Bloomington, IN.: National Education Service.

Senske, K. (2004). *Executive values: A Christian approach to organizational leadership.* Minneapolis, MN.: Augsburg Books.

Simpson, E. J. (1972). *The classification of educational objectives in the psychomotor domain: The psychomotor domain. Vol. 3.* Washington, DC: Gryphon House.

Sullivan , D. (1996). *How the best get better.* Toronto, Canada: The Strategic Coach, Inc.

Taylor, B. O. (2002). The effective schools process: Alive and well. *Phi Delta Kappan, 83*, 375-378.

Tomlinson, C. A. & Allan, S. D. (2000). *Leadership for differentiating schools & classrooms.* Alexandria, VA.: Association for Supervision and Curriculum Development.

Trump, J. L. & Baynham, D. (1961). *Guide to better schools.* Chicago, Il.: Rand McNally & Co.

Trump, J. L. (1977). *A School for Everyone.* Reston, VA.: The National Association of Secondary School Principals.

Waits, M. J., Campbell, H. E., Gau, R., Jacobs, E., Rex, T., & Hess, R. (2006). *Why some schools with Latino children beat the odds...and others don't.* Phoenix, AZ.: Center for the Future of Arizona.

Wasley, P. A. (2002). Small classes, small schools: The time is now. *Educational Leadership, 59*, 6-10.

Waters, J. T., Marzano, R. J., & McNulty, B. A. (2003). *Balanced leadership: What 30 years of research tells us about the effect of leadership on student achievement.* Aurora, CO: Mid-continent Research for Education and Learning.

Index

Page numbers followed by the letter "f" refer to figures.

190

About the Authors

Charles E. Ruebling
Principal Author

Dr. Ruebling is the Director of the Center for School Redesign, Vice President of The Ruebling Group, LLC, and an educational consultant.

During his 32-year career in education, Dr. Ruebling has served as an educational leader in Iowa and Minnesota and worked in an education related private sector business. His public school leadership assignments have included curriculum development, library/media programs, the application of educational technology, staff development, assessment programs, and teaching team leader. In the private sector, he led development and marketing for school administration and instructional management software products. Over the last decade, Dr. Ruebling has been a consultant focusing on curriculum, assessment, and leadership development; technology planning, and designing information systems for managing curriculum and instruction.

Dr. Ruebling is a past president of the Iowa Educational Media Association and the North Iowa Chapter of Phi Delta Kappa, was appointed by the governor to the Minnesota Elementary/Secondary/Vocational Computer Council, which he chaired, was elected to the TIES (Regional Computer Center) Board of Directors and Executive Committee, and served on the Eden Prairie (MN) Board of Education.

Dr. Ruebling received a Bachelor of Science degree in Mathematics, a Master of Science degree in Guidance and Counseling, and a Ph.D. degree in Educational Administration, all from Iowa State University. He can be contacted at The Center for School Redesign, 2672 Blackwater Road NW, Longville, MN 56655. Phone: 218-682-3392. E-mail: chuck@rueblinggroup.com.

Nancy A. Clarke
Collaborating Author

Mrs. Clarke is an educational consultant working with school districts and charter schools to improve the skills of teachers and administrators in the areas of curriculum, assessment, instruction, and leadership.

Mrs. Clarke's leadership in schools includes curriculum development, special education, state and federal program, testing, gifted education, staff development, Title I programs, and elementary school principal. In 1991, she was recognized as an Outstanding Principal in Maricopa County, Arizona.

Mrs. Clarke was a district administrator for the Cave Creek Unified School District in Cave Creek, Arizona. Her responsibilities included curriculum coordinator, special education director, State and Federal projects director, testing coordinator, and staff developer. Prior to this position, she was an elementary principal, gifted program developer and teacher, Title I program developer/teacher and a classroom teacher. Mrs. Clarke's consulting work includes membership on the Iowa State University School Improvement Model Team working in school districts across the country developing curriculum and assessment aligned with state standards. She is a member of the Arizona Department of Education Solutions Team evaluating the implementation of curriculum in failing schools. She has served as an adjunct instructor for Northern Arizona University teaching classroom assessment.

Mrs. Clarke is a past President of Public Education Partnership, a 501 C3 non-profit organization which raises money for community education; after school and summer programs; fine arts education; and mini-grants for teachers in the Cave Creek (AZ) Unified School District. With others, she has published articles in *Charter School Monthly*, Iowa *Educational Leadership*, *The Educational Forum*, and *Clearing House*.

Mrs. Clarke received a Bachelor of Arts degree in Elementary Education from Michigan State University, a Master of Arts degree in Curriculum and Instruction from San Diego State University, and a Master of Arts degree in Special Education/ focus gifted education from Arizona State University. She can be contacted at P.O. Box 3156, Carefree, AZ 85377. Phone: 480-488-9266. E-mail: rnclarke37@dancris.com.

Frances A. Kayona
Collaborating Author

Dr. Kayona, is an associate professor in the Department of Educational Leadership and Community Psychology at St. Cloud State University in St. Cloud, Minnesota. She teaches courses in advanced supervision, program evaluation, personnel administration, curriculum development, research design, and organizational theory.

Dr. Kayona served as the assistant director, research associate, and consultant for the School Improvement Model Research Center at Iowa State University in Ames As a consultant to project school districts, Dr. Kayona led teachers in the development of standards-based curriculum and assessment for all content area. She also worked with stakeholders and school administrators developing performance evaluation systems for teachers, administrators, and support and classified staff, with an emphasis on the use of 360-degree feedback.

Dr. Kayona has traveled widely throughout the People's Republic of China where she taught conversational English for middle school students living in Xinjiang Province. Dr. Kayona is co-editor of copyrighted publications of standards-based curricula and criterion-referenced assessments in language arts and mathematics. She has presented on the topics of curriculum development and implementation and instructional leadership at the University Council for Educational Administration Conferences.

Dr. Kayona received a Bachelor of Arts degree in socio-cultural anthropology from Arizona State University and Masters of Science and Ph.D. degrees in Educational Leadership from Iowa State University. She can be contacted at St. Cloud University, A279 Education Building, St. Cloud, MN 56301. Phone:320-308-3170. E-mail: fakayona@stcloudstate.edu.

Shirley B. Stow
Collaborating Author

Dr. Stow is an educational consultant working to improve the educational environment in schools through effective leadership, the development of curricula and the appropriate assessments, and professional growth of teachers.

Dr. Stow's leadership in public schools includes classroom teacher grades 3-8, K-12 social studies department head, elementary school principal, and curriculum director. As an Associate Professor of Educational Administration at Iowa State University in Ames, she directed the field-based School Improvement Model Research Center for 25 years. Each year Dr. Stow works with numerous groups of educational professionals to improve their skills in curriculum, assessment, and leadership. She has worked at 65 project sites across the United States, in Canada, and in Western Europe. She has worked in the Department of Defense Dependents Schools in Panama and in the Taipei American School in Taiwan. And she has been a consultant to under performing schools in South Carolina and Arizona as well as Charter Schools.

Dr. Stow was honored to be selected to participate in the National Invitational Research Conference sponsored by the National Board for Professional Teaching Standards. She has received curriculum audit training and served on the steering committee of a Ford Foundation grant for planning educational television programs for Iowa students. Dr. Stow has written manuals and books and is published widely in journals. Selected books include *A Clinical Manual for Teacher Performance Evaluation* (with R. P. Manatt), a *Report for Developing and Testing a Model for Measuring and Improving Educational Outcomes* (with R. P. Manatt), various train-the-trainers manuals, and a *Technical Report of a Follow-Up Study* (which focused on the use of leadership skills). Selected articles include *A Systems Approach to Curriculum Development and Curriculum-Aligned Testing*, *Improving Student Learning: Lessons From the Filed* (with C. E. Ruebling, F. A. Kayona, and N. A. Clarke), and *Instructional Leadership: An Essential Ingredient for Improving Student Learning* (with C. E Ruebling, F.A Kayona, and N.A. Clarke).

Dr. Stow received a Bachelor of Science in Education degree in Elementary Education from Drake University; a Master of Science degree in Educational Administration, Elementary from Iowa State University; and a Ph.D. degree in Educational Administration (with emphasis on Curriculum) from Iowa State University. She can be contacted at 2829 Buckingham Court, Ames, IA 50010. Phone: 515-232-6584. E-mail: sbstow@qwest.net.

194

Printed in the United States
67186LVS00005B/93

9 781425 959715